PARTAKE

TO CONNECT THE POWER IN THE HOLY

COMMUNI

ON

Ben Okorie

GADOL TECH.
CONSULT

Scripture quotations, are taken from the *King James Authorized Version (Old King James) (KJV) and The New Living Translation (NLT). Where otherwise, it is stated and indicated. Partake To Connect The Power In The Holy Communion.*

A spirit inspired resource to prepare and discipline the mind for outstanding success-God's Way.

ISBN: 978-978-781-959-3

Publish by GADOL TECH CONSULT

In association with:

SALVATION ASSURANCE & LIBERATION TABERNACLE (SALT)

An Outreach Ministry of Ben Okorie and family.

Email: bcokoriegreat@gmail.com

Printed in Nigeria.

DEDICATION

This divine project is dedicated to God the Father, God the Son, and God the Holy Spirit as always to Whom I owe the gratitude in the Communion of grace and truth

AND

The Church, the body of Christ to which I belong, and with which I am in a Communion of fellowship to worship the King of kings.

Let's keep partaking in full measure and wisdom, until He returns to receive us unto Himself.

- The Edenic Covenant

- The Adamic covenant

- The Noahic Covenant

4.   MAJOR TURNING POINT IN THE.

HISTORY OF GOD'S VISITATIONS IN

COVENANT RELATIONSHIPS WITH

MAN, THE RESEARCH INSIGHTS

- The Abrahamic Covenant

- The Mosaic Covenant

- The Palestinian Covenant

- The Davidic Covenant

5.   THE   RESEARCH   FORESIGHT-THE   NEW
COVENANT OF GRACE. (Now operational but still
looking ahead beyond now.)

6.   SUMMARY OF THE HIGHLIGHTS OF THE
COVENANTS AND THE RELATION OF CHRIST TO THEM.

7.   THE SEED OF THE REVELATION
(INNERMOST LAYER) THE SPIRITUAL
SIGNIFICANCE OF THE HOLY COMMUNION

8.   PROCLAIM, PARTAKE AND CONNECT

COMMUNION OF LIFE

PRACTICAL DIMENSION

9. EXAMINE YOURSELVES FOR UNWORTHINESS

10. GUIDELINES ON COMMUNION MATERIALS

11. EMPIRICAL, BIBLICAL AND CONTEMPORARY EVIDENCES OF LIFE

THE SANTUARY EFFECTS OF THE HOLY COMMUNION.

- ALTAR DEDICATIONS:
- 1ST DEDICATION BY MOSES (UNITY)
- 2ND DEDICATION BY DAVID (DIVINITY)
- 3RD DEDICATION BY SOLOMON (TRINITY)
- 4TH DEDICATION BY ELDERS & GENTILES (STABILITY)

12. (I) 5TH DEDICATION: OFFERING OF CHRIST AS THE PASSOVER LAMB: (GRACE)

6TH DEDICATION: OFFERING OF ONESELF TO CHRIST BY FAITH FOR SALVATION (MAN)

- 7TH DEDICATION: THE REBUILDING OF THE FALLEN AND REUINED TABERNACLE OF DAVIDE AND ITS DEDICATION (COMPLETION)

- 8TH DEDICATION: THE UNVEILING OF THE KINGDOM OF GOD, THE NEW JERUSALEM AFTER THE WHITE THRONE JUDGEMENT. (PERFECTION)

12.   (II)   INSPIRED EXPLICATIONS
- GENERAL COMMENTRIES
- SUMMARY.

ACKNOWLEDGMENT

My Lord And Savior Jesus Christ unto The Father.
For saving me to serve and blessing me to be a blessing even with the tongue as the pen of a ready writer inditing good matters in His presence.

THE HOLY SPIRIT.

How can I speak, if you had not spoken, write, if you have not written. In this holy work then lies, "thus says the Lord" and "It is written" to educate the mind and discipline it.
Grateful Lord.

Mr. Emmanuel Nwankwo:
He has remained committed and unrelenting. His rich spiritual insights have continued to check, add and reinforce. Thank you, Emma, a blessing you are and do show yourself friendly and a friend indeed and in need.

Messers Festus Ojukwu and Emmanuel Agu
My two special assistants and technical support staff, always sitting the work on the world of technology.

Wife Violet Nmema Okorie and daughter Gold Nmesoma Okorie.

Cheer leaders, providing all the needs of the body and encouragements to run without fainting. Don't faint too.

FOREWORD

INSPIRED!

BY THE HOLY SPIRIT AND ADVANCED BY HIM.

BACKGROUND

I was in the Spirit, worshiping the King of Kings in all the heavens and the earth, on Sunday, June 25th, 2023. At about 8:45am, I was hurrying to shower and get ready to take my Sunday, Sunday medicine, the Holy Communion, when I heard this in my spirit "It's also your sacrifice". True, I said, not knowing to whom or how. I needed to know more about this sacred ritual.

Sacrifice had been a recurring word that morning as I posted my daily message on social media, commenting on the sacrifice Job was performing for his children to atone for any presumptuous sins, which, to his mind, they may have probably committed against God while partying.

My take on the posted message was that it is better to prevent than to cure. What is the essence of allowing children to be partying all over the place, only to turn around and perform sacrifices to clean them up? With the scripture now in place and in the public domain, it is evident that excessive partying or revelling, implied in the narrative, is a work of the flesh. I therefore urged parents to do more to focus their children on

God rather than use their affluence to support their excesses, especially in these days of social media malaise.

It should be acknowledged, though, that the scriptures were not in place in the days of Job in the land of Luz.

That was the setting.
The lengthy and unfruitful discourse that Job had with his three friends was a devil-sponsored sacrifice 2.0 to themselves.

To be honest, Job and his friends were like Cornelius in Acts 10, who was worshipping God but needed to be taught the right and acceptable way, which God encouraged him to do by sending for Peter, who was in a nearby city.

The Jews thought they had it all put together until Jesus showed up and told them, based on their actions and behaviour, that Satan was their father and not Abraham or the God of Abraham, as they claimed.
They therefore needed to be saved, lest they perish in their sins.

The central message in all of the above is that we only know in part. Nobody knows it all. We need to submit ourselves to the instructions, corrections, rebukes, and reproofs of the Holy Spirit based on the doctrines and teachings of our Lord to gain wisdom and understanding in all aspects of life.

That's what revelation, which illuminates the mind with the truth, does each time to help our faith life. I eventually had my bath, took Holy Communion, and remained in the presence of God thereafter, reading and studying along the lines of what I heard.

It was not long before the heavens were opened to me, and I knew what the Lord wanted me to do with the encounter and revelation.

The light He flooded in my heart regarding the Holy Communion, taking me through scripture after scripture from the ages to date, gave birth to this project in one hour. It was like engaging in conventional research or being given an assignment, which it is in all its ramifications. Partake with me as I share, in faith and righteousness, my findings. Shalom!

Ben Okorie (Coordinator, Multiply Your Grace (MYG))

CHAPTER ONE

WHAT THE LORD SHOWED ME. THE SHELL (OUTER LAYER)

In John 4, Jesus told the Samaritan woman this:

Jesus replied, "Believe me, dear woman, the time is coming when it will no longer matter whether you worship the Father on this mountain or in Jerusalem. You Samaritans know very little about the one you worship, while we Jews know all about him, for salvation comes through the Jews. But the time is coming-indeed it's here now-when true worshipers will worship the Father in spirit and in truth. The Father is looking for those who will worship him that way. For God is Spirit, so those who worship him must worship in spirit and in truth." *(John 4:21-24 NLT)*

Here is what we get from the above statement of Jesus:

He acknowledged the deep dichotomy between the Jews and the Gentiles regarding true religion. The Time is coming when there will be a UNIFICATION of worship, a new Way entirely that will unify both the Jewish traditional way of worship and the heathen way of the gentiles. That centre of worship unto the Father, both in time and action, is Him, Jesus, as the Head of the Church that would result from the merger of the two as His body. He confirmed the above when he unequivocally asserted that that time was here already and those that will flow into Him as "True Worshipers" . He is the Truth. Knowledge is key in the new order, but not enough. Experience is necessary. It adds virtue to the knowledge of God. The woman was experiencing one as she was engrossed in that discussion with the Lord.

To confirm the above statement, He took me to yet other scriptures.

1. *2 Corinthians 8:7-8*
Therefore, as ye abound in every thing, in faith, and utterance, and knowledge, and in all diligence, and in your love to us, see that ye abound in this grace also. I speak not by commandment, but by occasion of the forwardness of others, and to prove the sincerity of your love.

2. In view of all this, make every effort to respond to God's promises. Supplement your faith with a generous provision of moral excellence, and moral excellence with knowledge, and knowledge with self-control, and self-control with patient

endurance, and patient endurance with godliness, and godliness with brotherly affection, and brotherly affection with love for everyone. The more you grow like this, the more productive and useful you will be in your knowledge of our Lord Jesus Christ. But those who fail to develop in this way are shortsighted or blind, forgetting that they have been cleansed from their old sins. *(2 Peter 1:5-9 NLT)*

The takeaway from the above two scriptures is that your knowledge of God should lead you to God in love; otherwise, you will be lost. There is a practical dimension to knowledge, and practicing it right brings the whole knowledge to light and bears fruit of righteousness.

The Samaritan woman knew something about worship, but Jesus took her to a whole new level.

What all these means is that there is something the Lord wants to show me about Holy Communion that will change our perspective on the knowledge and practice of it, as well as resolve some myths around it, to deepen our faith in Him as true worshippers.

I then delved further, like a man on a mission, to research and postulate with the word and the Holy Spirit as my guide and guard.

Is that not what we do in conventional research? First, a research area is identified, and a topic is chosen to dig in and pull out our knowledge of facts and figures. They are then reviewed in light of existing and previously held opinions and positions. New facts and trends that will push the frontiers of knowledge are noted, posited, and posted for all to learn and adjust to shape new behaviours and actions, provided they are consistent, provable and reliable to educate, inform and transform, that's what happens on the sacred plane too, and that's the approach we are adopting here. Research in both planes connects the past and present and establishes the future. What research is to the secular world, revelation is to the sacred. Men copied research methodology from God Himself, as would be established in this work. All wisdom in righteousness is from God.

HOLY COMMUNION OR THE LORD'S SUPPER AS RECORDED IN THE GOSPELS

The Shell of the Revelation.

1.   **EVANGELIST MATTHEW: (Jesus as King of Heaven & Earth)**

As they were eating, Jesus took some bread and blessed it. Then he broke it in pieces and gave it to the disciples, saying, "Take this and eat it, for this is my body." And he took a cup of wine and gave thanks to God for it. He gave it to them and said, "Each of you drink from it, for this is my blood, which confirms the covenant between God and his people. It is poured out as a sacrifice to forgive the sins of many. Mark my words-I will not drink wine again until the day I drink it new with you in my Father's Kingdom." *(Matthew 26:26-29 NLT)*

2.   EVANGELIST MARK: (Jesus as Servant)

As they were eating, Jesus took some bread and blessed it. Then he broke it in pieces and gave it to the disciples, saying, "Take it, for this is my body." And he took a cup of wine and gave thanks to God for it. He gave it to them, and they all drank from it. And he said to them, "This is my blood, which confirms the covenant between God and his people. It is poured out as a sacrifice for many. I tell you the truth, I will not drink wine again until the day I drink it new in the Kingdom of God." *(Mark 14:22-25 NLT)*

3.   EVANGELIST LUKE (Jesus as Son of man)

When the time came, Jesus and the apostles sat down together at the table. Jesus said, "I have been very eager to eat this Passover meal with you before my suffering begins. For I tell you now that I won't eat this meal again until its meaning is fulfilled in the Kingdom of God." Then he took a cup of wine and gave thanks to God for it. Then he said, "Take this and share it among yourselves. For I will not drink wine again until the Kingdom of God has come." He took some bread and gave thanks to God for it. Then he broke it in pieces and gave it to the disciples, saying, "This is my body, which is given for you. Do this in remembrance of me." After supper he took another cup of wine and said, "This cup is the new covenant between God and his people-an agreement confirmed with my blood, which is poured out as a sacrifice for you. *(Luke 22:14-20 NLT)*

Please note the following with respect to the account of Evangelist Luke before we share the account of St. John:

He captured vividly that there were two
meals in the evening of the last supper.
The regular Supper and

The Lord's Supper
The use of the words 'after Supper', and 'another cup'
supports this view.

He captured the Lord's command that the disciples were to continue to do it IN REMEMBRANCE of Him.

He described the cup of the blood of Jesus as a COVENANT of SACRIFICE between God and His people, poured out. The Cup of the Blood of Jesus is therefore a TESTIMONY that speaks blessing; hence, it is also called the "Cup of Blessings."

All three Evangelists agree on this point.

4.   SAINT JOHN (Jesus as the Son of God Or God)

John captures the Lord's Supper in a very unusual manner, unlike the other synoptic gospels.

Hence, I have chosen to address him as 'Saint' instead of 'Evangelist ' to distinguish him.

It is my invention. They are all Evangelists and Saints of the Lord.

The following scene between the Lord and His disciples, supposedly referencing the same "Last Supper," focused primarily on what happened to the disciple who betrayed Jesus, Judas, rather than what Jesus told the whole group of disciples, as reported by the synoptic gospels (Matthew, Mark, and Luke). Perhaps this is to show the full picture of what transpired that night, as well as the potency of that ritual. Now Jesus was deeply troubled, and he exclaimed, "I tell you the truth, one of you will betray me!" The disciples looked at each other, wondering whom he could mean. The disciple Jesus loved was sitting next to Jesus at the table. Simon Peter motioned to him to ask, "Who's he talking about?" So that disciple leaned over to Jesus and asked, "Lord, who is it?" Jesus responded, "It is the one to whom I give the bread I dip in the bowl." And when he had dipped it, he gave it to Judas, son of Simon Iscariot. When Judas had eaten the bread, Satan entered into him. Then Jesus told him, "Hurry and do what you're going to do." None of the others at the table knew what Jesus meant. Since Judas was their treasurer, some thought Jesus was telling him to go and pay for the food or to give some money to the poor. So Judas left at once, going out into the night. *John 13:21-30 NLT*

In the above peculiar reportage, note:

1.	Jesus was aware that the one who would betray Him was among them, just like how Satan was present in the garden and led the chosen ones to commit sin by eating the forbidden fruit. It is possible that the Serpent was also present on Noah's ark as one of the unclean animals.

2. Other disciples did not know that there was an enemy within until he was revealed by Jesus, probably to only one (John) and at most two (John and Peter). Note therefore that "Only God can reveal and punish sin, which man may not even be aware of". You can ask God to reveal the sin in your life and in your midst for knowledge and caution, and ask for forgiveness. Based on the word standard, you may know your sin, as Judas probably knew his, but not the sin of others, lest you stumble.

3. Holy Communion has a dual role as a discerner of the intent of man, leading to either life or death, much the same way as the Word of the Lord judges' men, as the double-edged sword of the Spirit (More on this later).

MORE KNOWLEDGE REVEALED

Earlier, St. John recorded a deeper understanding of the Lord's elaborate discourse in a conference with the disciples regarding the significant importance and purpose of taking Holy Communion, represented by the bread as His body and the wine as His blood. None of the three

Evangelists captured this elaborate teaching on Holy Communion, as a figure of His sacrifice for our sins.

Watch!

"I tell you the truth, anyone who believes has eternal life. Yes, I am the bread of life! Your ancestors ate manna in the wilderness, but they all died. Anyone who eats the bread from heaven, however, will never die. I am the living bread that came down from heaven. Anyone who eats this bread will live forever; and this bread, which I will offer so the world may live, is my flesh." Then the people began arguing with each other about what he meant. "How can this man give us his flesh to eat?" they asked. So Jesus said again, "I tell you the truth, unless you eat the flesh of the Son of Man and drink his blood, you cannot have eternal life within you. But anyone who eats my flesh and drinks my blood has eternal life, and I will raise that person at the last day. For my flesh is true food, and my blood is true drink. Anyone who eats my flesh and drinks my blood remains in me, and I in him. I live because of the living Father who sent me; in the same way, anyone who feeds on me will live because of me. I am the true bread that came down from heaven. Anyone who eats this bread will not die as your ancestors did (even though they ate the manna) but will live forever." He said these things while he was teaching in the synagogue in Capernaum. (*John 6:47-59 NLT*)

In the following great teaching of our Lord, the following are action and wisdom points to take away: The bread represents the body of Jesus, and the wine is His blood, just as Jesus is the Word made flesh. Both are described as true food and true drink, not in the regular sense, but as symbols of Holy Communion in covenant relationship with God in Christ. Partaking in the Holy Communion signifies that one is in a covenant relationship with God, which delivers eternal life to him. The reverse is also true. If you don't eat it, you do not have eternal life. Jesus says so, looking ahead to confessing Him as your Lord and Saviour, which the communion symbolises in teaching at that time. Taking Holy Communion is therefore a way to testify that one believes that Jesus is the Messiah, and through Him, you receive a new life in abundance and eternally. It is a faith affirmation. The eating of the flesh of Jesus and drinking of his blood (The Holy Communion) is indicated to be a continuous exercise. He kept using the action verbs 'eats' and 'drinks' in their present continuous tenses. I believe this alludes to what He said in Luke, saying, "For I will not drink wine again until the Kingdom of God has come." *Luke 22:18 NLT*

"Keep, eating my flesh, keep drinking my blood, IN REMEMBRANCE of The SACRIFICE on the cross, until the marriage supper or wedding feast of the Lamb in the new Kingdom. (Rev.19:9).

Put succinctly, it means "Keep believing, keep looking forward to the marriage supper until it happens- Be steadfast"

Perhaps the absence or near absence of teachings on this subject, like the matter of the cross, must have accounted for its neglect, to which the Lord is drawing our attention. This could also account for the poor state of mind of some who partake without discernment, as well as the discontent, just as it greeted Jesus' announcement that He is the bread of life that should be eaten.

More research is indicated. Let's dig deeper.

CHAPTER TWO

WHAT THE LORD SHOWED ME, THE KERNEL. (THE MIDDLE LAYER) ADDITIONAL PERSPECTIVES)

We have shared in chapter 1 above, perspectives from the three synoptic gospels as well as the peculiar reportage of St. John, not only in that great teaching highlighting the symbolic significance of the Holy Communion as the source of eternal life but also the role it played in the life of Judas, who betrayed him. Please note now that Jesus Christ is the source of that eternal life. The Holy Communion is a symbol or a token of it, evidencing your faith in Him as the source of that life. To further illustrate: The teller or receipt you get when you carry out a transaction in the bank is just the evidence of the transaction, not the transaction itself.

In this chapter, we will highlight one more perspective in revelation to yet another apostle whom the Lord encountered after He had left the earth.

APOSTLE & EVANGELIST PAUL (Jesus as God in Heaven - Glorified)

For I pass on to you what I received from the Lord himself. On the night when he was betrayed, the Lord Jesus took some bread and gave thanks to God for it. Then he broke it in pieces and said, "This is my body, which is given for you. Do this in remembrance of me." In the same way, he took the cup of wine after supper, saying, "This cup is the new covenant between God and his people-an agreement confirmed with my blood. Do this in remembrance of me as often as you drink it." For every time you eat this bread and drink this cup, you are announcing the Lord's death until he comes again. So anyone who eats this bread or drinks this cup of the Lord unworthily is guilty of sinning against the body and blood of the Lord. That is why you should examine yourself before eating the bread and drinking the cup. For if you eat the bread or drink the cup without honoring the body of Christ, you are eating and drinking God's judgment upon yourself. That is why many of you are weak and sick and some have even died. But if we would examine ourselves, we would not be judged by God in this way. Yet when we are judged by the Lord, we are being disciplined so that we will not be condemned along with the world. *(1 Corinthians 11:23-32 NLT)*

I am persuaded to believe that Apostle Paul must have reviewed the practice of partaking in the Lord's Supper and went to the Lord to receive a fresh and direct word to strengthen the practice of this very strong pillar of the Christian faith.

Don't just take my word for it. Hear him: "For I pass on to you what I received from the Lord Himself."

The emphasis is clear. He neither learned it nor read it from anybody or anywhere. He received it directly from the Lord. It was a personal, elaborate revelation to him, probably in response to a question or inquiry he made to the Lord on the matter.

The Lord Himself was pleased to reveal to him what the true position was, not because what He revealed before was not true, but because the practice of it had become so irreverent that it needed to be reviewed, to obviate spiritual damage both to the believer and the Church. (That's the judgment dimension, not for condemnation but for rebuke.)

In the revelation, the following truths were uncovered: 1. It happened on the night when He was betrayed, **AFTER THE REGULAR SUPPER.** The communion therefore played a role of separation between the righteous and the wicked. This is evident when you compare what happened to the other disciples on the one hand and Judas on the other, as St. John captured it. (More on this later.)

2.   The communion, or Lord's Supper, is a token of the new covenant (agreement) between God and His people, confirmed or sealed with His blood.

3.   The Holy Communion should be taken in REMEMBRANCE of the Lord and as OFTEN as you can partake. This is the thanksgiving dimension for salvation.

4.   Each time you partake in the Lord's Supper, you also declare or announce His death until He comes. This is the mourning dimension of deliverance and comfort. In this way, taking Holy
Communion is a way of keeping your faith and
hope in Christ alive until He returns. *(See Matt.
5:4; John 16:33)*.

5.   Taking the Holy Communion without discerning that It Is the body and blood of the Lord (understanding the significance and symbolism) is deemed to have eaten it unworthily. This is eating and drinking judgment upon oneself, which can result in weakness, sickness, or even death because it is sin against oneself and against the Lord. The death here is not a condemnation to hell but an extreme rebuke to a believer.

Based on these 5 revelations above, it is very dangerous for those who have not believed in the Lord (unbelievers) or those who are presumptuous, presuming they understand when they don't, or living in known sin, though they are believers, to take Holy Communion.

The Apostle Paul says, If you want to avoid being disciplined by the Lord as a presumptive or irreverent believer or being condemned together with the unbelieving world, examine yourself and possibly make peace with God. This includes believing in and confessing Jesus as your Lord and Saviour, seeking understanding, and/or repenting of your sin.

I believe in all of my heart that Judas Iscariot falls into the category of presumptive believers, who most probably thought that he understood the things of the Spirit, undermining the power of the Holy Communion as the discerner of the intent of men. He was in sin by planning to betray the Lord and taking part in the Lord's Supper, which represents the body and blood of the

Holy One of Israel. They don't work together.

Though there was nothing he could have done at this time to change the predetermined counsel of God, that he was that son of perdition, he should have sought counsel after hearing those words repeatedly from the Lord, regarding the significance of the bread and the wine. Better still, he could have repented, though he wouldn't have been based on the irreversibility of scripture (Psalm 8). However, his reward for his role in betraying the Lord, is damning and stands as stipulated in the scriptures.

It is now a big warning to us believers, as Apostle Paul posited, to avoid this hypocritical danger in the practice of our faith in this regard. The Communion revealed the heart of Judas, as a chamber prepared for Satan to come in and facilitate his wicked plan of conspiracy with the chief priests to betray the Lord of Glory.

Watch!

Jesus responded, "It is the one to whom I give the bread I dip in the bowl." And when he had dipped it, he gave it to Judas, son of Simon Iscariot. When Judas had eaten the bread, Satan entered into him. Then Jesus told him, "Hurry and do what you're going to do." *(John 13:26-27 NLT).*

It is a warning to anyone who would think that you can be presumptuous, live in sin, and partake in the most sacred act with the Lord. Scripture says, The wicked do not know where they stumble.

Even in the civil judicial process, you can't bait and aid, probate, and arbitrate at the same time in the same matter.

To buttress this truth, Apostle Paul asked those who partake in the cup of blessing as well as the communion with sacrifices to the idols if they are more powerful than the Lord. No one should ever imagine or dare.

Watch!

If you think you are standing strong, be careful not to fall. So, my dear friends, flee from the worship of idols. You are reasonable people. Decide for yourselves if what I am saying is true. When we bless the cup at the Lord's Table, aren't we sharing in the blood of Christ? And when we break the bread, aren't we sharing in the body of Christ? And though we are many, we all eat from one loaf of bread, showing that we are one body. Think about the people of Israel. Weren't they united by eating the sacrifices at the altar? What am I trying to say? Am I saying that food offered to idols has some significance, or that idols are real gods? No, not at all.

I am saying that these sacrifices are offered to demons, not to God. And I don't want you to participate with demons. You cannot drink from the cup of the Lord and from the cup of demons, too. You cannot eat at the Lord's Table and at the table of demons, too. What? Do we dare to rouse the Lord's jealousy? Do you think we are stronger than he is? *(1 Corinthians 10:12, 14-22 NLT).*

You see, Apostle Paul certainly observed something with respect to the intricacies of this holy ritual, and sought the Lord in prayer for more revelations, which he thus set in order above. These revelations were not evident in the foregoing accounts of the four disciples of Jesus Christ, who partook in the very last Holy Communion the Lord had with the apostles, except Luke, who was not an apostle.

His work, like the one I am doing now, was the product of revelatory research in wisdom and understanding.

The truth is that, it is like that in virtually all our dealings with God. More are revealed as we advance steadily along the line of faith, beholding that light, thus diminishing what lies behind and making glorious what lies ahead. *(See proverb 4:18; 2 Corinthians 3:16-18.)*

Before we embark further in this, journey and to avoid believing the lie of the devil, that you are being bored with unnecessary details, keep in mind what the Lord told me that fateful morning: "Communion is a Sacrifice or a covenant. "We are therefore being led by the Holy Spirit in a divine research to establish this truth in our hearts, boost and deepen our faith in Christ through partaking in the Holy Communion-the Cup of Blessing.

Let's connect the past and the future, too.

CHAPTER THREE

COVENANT PERSPECTIVES- THE HINDSIGHT, INSIGHT AND FORESIGHT OF THE REVELATION- (THE RESEARCH)

HINDSIGHT.

According to Scofield reference notes in the King James Life Study Bible, there were seven covenants before the emergence of the new covenant, referred to by Jesus in that last Supper with His disciples, making them eight in all.

Eight (8), as we know, spiritually stands for a new beginning. Those eight covenants and their corresponding scripture references are:

1. EDENIC Genesis 1:28
2. ADAMIC Genesis 3:15
3. NOAHIC Genesis 9:1
4. ABRAHAMIC Genesis 15:18
5. MOSAIC Exodus 19:25
6. PALESTINIAN Deuteronomy 30:3

7. DAVIDIC, 2 Samuel 7:16
8. NEW Hebrews 8:8

Covenant is a very huge concept, morally, socially, legally, and above all, spiritually.

In fact, life is generally about covenant relationships. This is true, whether it is in business, marriage, ministry, or government between man and man, nation and nation, or God and man. My mission here is not to delve into this huge and complex topic, even in its spiritual context and depth, with all the intricacies to fill our heads with all the diverse notions across those eight covenants.

I will situate our discourse to suit the revelation I received from the Lord on the subject of Holy Communion.

According to the Easton Bible Dictionary, a covenant is "A contract or an agreement between two parties".

The Hebrew word for covenant is 'bèriyth' or 'berith'. It is derived from a root word that means "to cut." A covenant in that spiritual sense is a 'cutting, alluding to the cutting into two animals, with the contracting parties to the contract agreement passing between them. This was the setting for what happened in

Genesis, where God Almighty entered into a covenant relationship with Abraham. (More on this under "Insight")

Though the word covenant occurred for the first time in Genesis 6, where God spoke to Noah that He would establish His covenant with him, covenant is as old as creation itself. What happened between God and Adam was a covenant relationship in which God created and bequeathed the earth to man under a non-formal covenant arrangement. This is different from what happened in Genesis chapter 9, where God formally entered into a covenant relationship with Noah, representing the new world after the judgment of the flood.

With hindsight, looking at Rom. 5:12-19, there was a covenant of Works or nature, by which God placed Adam in the Garden of Eden; hence, it is called:

EDENIC COVENANT

Here are the essential components of that covenant relationship:

PARTIES God was the Moral Governor.

Adam was the free moral agent capable of making a choice and representing all natural creations in posterity.

TERMS AND CONDITIONS

Perfect obedience to God's law. *(Matt 19:16-17)*

REWARD:

Life for obedience, symbolised by the tree of life (not to be eaten),
Death for disobedience, symbolised by the tree of knowledge of good and evil (not to be eaten)

The alternate names for this covenant are:
Covenant of nature because it was made with man in his unfallen state or during the dispensation of innocence.

OR

Covenant of life because "life" was its promise and reward for perfect obedience.

OR

Legal Covenant because perfect obedience was its condition to inherit the promised life. In conventional law, a breach by any of the parties Is grounds to make the contract void or voidable.

"Tree of Life" is therefore its seal and symbol, which is Our Lord Jesus in figure.
It's a known fact, because man disobeyed God and ate the tree of knowledge of good and evil, he was banished from Eden out of the reach of the Tree of Life, and, as such, without the life of

God. He inherited the life of the deceiver, Satan, who deceived him into disobeying God.

Thus, the contract between God and the man Adam, to some degree, became void.

CHAPTER FOUR

MAJOR TURNING POINT IN THE HISTORY OF GOD'S VISITATIONS IN COVENANT RELATIONSHIPS WITH MAN - THE ABRAHAMIC COVENANT

INSIGHT

After the fall of man, there were other intervening and remedial covenants, such as the:

Adamic, the 2nd (Era of conscience after innocence in which the seed of the woman that will crush Satan that caused the disobedience of Adam was promised, and an animal was killed to inaugurate the covenant),

Noahic, the 3rd (Era of human government, with man now allowed to take animal meat but without blood, and empowered judicially to judge and take the life of any, both man and beast, that sheds blood of the innocent)

Then the 4th Covenant:

THE ABRAHAMIC COVENANT

Following the institution of human government under the Noahic Covenant *(Gen. 9:1-6)*, God permitted man to govern himself and the world on His behalf. He also empowered man to judicially take the life of any man or beast that sheds blood of the innocent.

Every governmental duty and responsibility in the administration of her people rests on this authority, even to this day. However, it is a known fact that the mixed race of both the Semitic (the Middle East race) and non-Semitic people (the rest of the races), as it were, governed for themselves and not for God, just as it still does to this day by the governments of the world. The racial testing of the conscience as well as the fairness of man in justice ended in the confusion of the tongue in the building of the tower of Babel, recorded in Genesis 11.

The need for the separation of the Semitic (God's own people, the descendants of Shem committed to God), and the heathen, (the rest of the people of the world), arose and began. This is God's birthing research methodology in pursuit of a defined goal, as we referenced earlier.

In research, you need to narrow the search for answers to your questions from the population to a sample, which is a defined portion of the entire population. The same approach is adopted in any strategic investigation.

 All these are words of wisdom copied from God.

The search for the seed of the woman spoken of in *Gen. 3:15,* under the Adamic covenant, Who would accomplish God's desire to crush the head of the Serpent, progressed with this separation in the Noahic covenant.

God found for Himself, as He did Noah, a friend called Abram (whom He renamed Abraham) after the dispensation of the Noahic covenant ended with the failure of human government. He groomed and walked Abraham into the 4th Covenant, which gave birth to the dispensation of PROMISE.

Four (4) is the spiritual number of stability (North, South, East, and West).

A dispensation is the privilege that a covenant guarantees and underpins.

It was innocence under the Edenic, conscience under the Adamic, Human government under the Noahic, and now Promise under the Abrahamic covenant.

In this covenant, God hinted to Abraham that in him all the families of the earth (North, South, East, and West) would be blessed.

Further details as to how this feat would be achieved are stated below.

FORMATION OF THE COVENANT

A. God encounters Abram *(Gen12:1-4)*
B. God confirms and reassures Abram or Abraham *(Gen 13:14–17, 15:1–7; 17:1–8)*.

The major distinct parts and highlights of this fourth Covenant are:

PARTIES:

God is the Promisor or Promiser (The Undertaker) under the covenant.

Abraham and his descendants are the promisees or heirs to the promise.

MAJOR COMPONENTS OF THE PROMISE

(Gen.12:1-4)

1. "I will make of thee a great nation." Fulfilled in three principal ways:

a. In the natural posterity, as the dust of the earth *(Gen 13:16; John 8:37)*, which refers to the Hebrew nation out of Abraham

b. In spiritual posterity, "look now toward heaven; so shall your seed be." *(John 8:39; Rom. 4:16–17; 9:7-8; Gal. 3:6-7, 29)*

c. Ishmael also had a share of the natural prosperity in property, not posterity, indicating the universality of the promise (all the people of the earth). *(Gen17:18-20)*

2. "I will bless thee." Fulfilled in two ways:

A. Temporally *(Gen 13:14-15, 17; 15:18; 24:34-35)*

B. spiritually *(Gen.15:6, John8:56)*

3. "And make thy name great."

Abraham is one of the Universal household names.

4. "And thou shall be a blessing."

(Gal.3:13-14)

5. "I will bless them that bless thee."

See '6' below on how fulfilled it is in relation to it.

6. "I will curse him that curseth thee."

History reveals and confirms that persecutors of the Jews have received their due share of ill will. The opposite is also true. *(Deut. 30:7; Is. 14:1; Joel 3:1-8;*

Micah 5:7-9; Haggai 2:22; Zech. 14:1-3; Matt 25:40, 45)

7. "In thee shall all the nations be blessed." In the 7th dimension of this mega promise, there was an allusion to Christ and a reference to the Adamic Covenant regarding the offspring or seed of that woman that would crush the Serpent. *Gen.3:15*

This promise was fulfilled in Christ as that seed of Abraham, in and by Whom all the families of the earth (Jews and Gentiles) are blessed. *(Gal.3:16; John 8:56:58)*

NOTE:

1. The natural prosperity of the Jews was anchored on being given the promised land, flowing with milk and honey.

However, they had been dispossessed of that land in three dispersals and had been restored twice based on prophecy

a. Dispersed to Egypt, not as a nation but as a people, and restored. In Egypt, they lost the blessing but not the covenant. God remembered them and, by grace, raised Moses to rescue or deliver them.

b. Dispersed to Babylon and restored, God favoured them, using the Kings of the nation like

Cyrus, et al. *(Gen 15:13-14, 16; Jer. 25:11-12; Deut. 28:62-65; 30:1-3)*

c. Dispersed to all the nations of the world, restoration has begun gradually as Jews return to their homeland Israel, but would be fully achieved as in the exodus, when their Brother, the Messiah, would return as King under the Davidic Covenant (The 7th) to gather them from all corners of the world where they had been dispersed due to their stubbornness in rebellion. *(Deut. 30:3; Jer. 23:5-8; Ez. 37:21-25; Luke 1:30-33; Acts 15:14-17)*

TERMS AND CONDITIONS

When God encountered Abram in Gen. 12, He made no mention of any Condition to obtain His promised blessing. This was because His Son, the seed, an embodiment of grace and truth, was visibly in the picture. However, when Abram walked disorderly, God says: Walk before me and be perfect: meaning "follow, trust, and focus on me." The Abrahamic covenant is thus a near unconditional covenant, if not one entirely. It was a rebuke, not a condition to obtain the promise.

TOKEN:

Abraham and every male child, freeborn or slave born or bought with money, of the Jews must be circumcised on the foreskin of their genitals on the 8th day of his birth. Otherwise, such a male child shall be cut off from the people. *(Gen 17:11-14)*

Thus, for the first time, man was to bear on his body the emblem of consecration to God. In this, cutting, which is symbolic of a covenant, blood is shed in sacrifice.

Hitherto, it was the killing of animals under the first three covenants, plus a seven colour rainbow introduced after the judgment of the flood, by which God vowed to Noah and his children that He would no longer destroy all flesh and beasts by water.

The Abrahamic covenant provided much insight into the mind of God with respect to the search for the seed of the woman to crush the head of the Serpent.

Please read the prescribed scriptures to gain deeper insights into this covenant that opened the gateway of faith beyond what Noah experienced from and with God.

We are, however, constrained to review briefly, from the perspective of Scofield reference notes, another three covenants, the 5th, the 6th, and the 7th, before we open up to the 8th in pursuit of the seed of the woman, which liberated man from the bondage of sin.

That 8th, which will free man from sin, is symbolized in the circumcision of every male Hebrew child on the 8th day of birth.

The Abrahamic Covenant gave way partially to the 5th, 6th, and 7th Covenants. It is partial because it continues to underpin the basic principles of subsequent covenants. Its rejection, wittingly or unwittingly by the Israelites, vitiated the benefits and gave rise to subsequent covenants without ending the covenant itself. It is, however, all part of the divine plan of God to reveal what damage the devil did to him, as the works were finished from the foundation of the world. None took God by surprise.

The dispensation of PROMISE under the Abrahamic covenant ended when Israel rashly demonstrated human power to do the Will of God on their way to the promised land. They willfully accepted the law instead of remaining under grace, which the Abrahamic covenant connotes.

Watch!

Exodus 19:4-8: Ye have seen what I did unto the Egyptians, and how I bare you on eagles' wings, and brought you unto myself.

Now therefore, if ye will obey my voice indeed, and keep my covenant, then ye shall be a peculiar treasure unto me above all people: for all the earth is mine.

And ye shall be unto me a kingdom of priests, and an holy nation. These are the words which thou shalt speak unto the children of Israel. And Moses came and called for the elders of the people, and laid before their faces all these words which the LORD commanded him.

And all the people answered together, and said, All that the LORD hath spoken we will do. And Moses returned the words of the people unto the LORD.

In the next chapter (Exodus 20), God rolled out the commandments, and that was the beginning of the Isrealites undoing in sin and death. Mercy took flight through the window of grace, and the gavel entered. Every sin must be judged and punished according to the consecrated, holy law of God.

Then he added, "Now go and learn the meaning of this Scripture: 'I want you to show mercy, not offer sacrifices.' For I have come to call not those who think they are righteous, but those who know they are sinners." (Matthew 9:13 NLT)

Thus the dispensation of promise gave way to the dispensation of law to birth the

5TH COVENANT - THE MOSAIC (After the name Moses),

who was prepared by grace to lead the children of Israel to Canaan, the promised land.

However, the law did not abrogate the Abrahamic covenant, which is eternal (though it operated under a new symbolic covenant). *Gal.3:15-18.* Remember, it is in the Abrahamic Covenant that the Seed, a reference to Jesus Christ, is mentioned for the first time. That connects it directly to the prophecy about the seed of the woman in *Genesis 3:15.*

The law was a temporary disciplinary measure for the Israelites "Till the Seed come, to Whom the promise was made" *(Gal. 3:19-29; 4:1-7).*

The Mosaic Covenant is the fifth in the series and the first outside the book of Genesis, thus indicating the historic riches of that book of beginnings as well as a turning point in covenant relationships, opening a new vista.

The three major parts of the Mosaic Covenant are:

1. The commandments: expressing the righteous will of God for man to observe (Exod. 20:1–26)
2. Judgments: governing the social life of Israel, indicating rewards for obedience and punishment for disobedience. (Exo. 21:1–24:11). Not going to happen, man, was in his fallen state. Only mercy and grace would help.
3. Ordinances: governing the religious life of Israel (Exo. 31:18)

All these three forms "the Law" as generically used in the New Testament, e.g., *Matt 5:17-18. The commandments and the ordinances formed the religious system of Israel.*

TERMS AND CONDITIONS

1. complete and total observance of the whole ten commandments, without which there would be no reward. A failure in one is a failure in all, and reward is lost.

The law thus makes a demand on the will, emotions, and resources of the people, which they could not afford in their fallen state.

"BE CAREFUL WHAT YOU ASK FOR: KNOW YOUR STRENGTH AND WEAKNESS."

TOKEN

A major feature of the religious worship under the Mosaic Covenant is the appointment of a High priest to represent the people before Jehovah and the sacrifice of animals (lamb, sheep, oxen, or bulls) without blemish to provide "Cover" in atonement for their sins.

This sacrifice, which increased with sin following the introduction of the law, was in anticipation of the cross, where the needed acquittal from sin took place.

All the while, none of the covenants up until the new covenant with grace as the dispensation could acquit man of sin. Innocence was lost, conscience would either accuse or excuse, human government was abused and characterised by injustice and self-seeking, promise was despised and diminished, and now law was flagrantly disobeyed.

The immediate and remote consequences of the disobedience of the Israelites to the commandments of God, foreseen even before they entered the promised land, resulted in the **6TH COVENANT,** which Scofield chose to tag **THE PALESTINIAN** Covenant. " probably because it was entered into not by choice but by necessity. Its purpose was to further check the irreverent behaviour of the Jews, even before they inherited the land. Furthermore, the fact that the stock of the Jews, now about to enter the land, was primarily raised in the desert following the deaths of all those that originally left Egypt (except Joshua and Caleb), due to unfaithfulness to the Lord, necessitated the need to renew the laws and upgrade the consequences. The covenant was made in the land of the Palestines, hence the name.

THE PALESTINIAN COVENANT (6TH)

Highlights of this covenant, which sets out the conditions under which they entered the land, are:

1. Dispersion for disobedience *(Deut. 30:1; 28:63-68)*
2. Future repentance of Israel while on dispersion is foreseen *(Deut. 30:2).*

3. Return of the Lord foreseen *(Deut. 30:3; Amos 9:9-14; Acts 15:14-17)*

This will happen at the time of the reign of King David, and open the door for the 7th Covenant.

4. Restoration to the land following their repentance and God's mercy under the unconditional Abrahamic covenant *(Deut. 30:5; Is. 11:11-12; Jer. 23:3-8; Ezek 37:2125)*

5. National Conversion *(Deut. 30:6; Rom. 11:26-27; Hos. 2:14-16)*

6. Judgment of the nations that oppressed Israel while on dispersal *(Deut. 30:7; Is. 14:1-2; Joel 3:1-8; Matt. 25:31-46)*

7. National prosperity after repentance, restoration, conversion, and judgment of their oppressors as a nation possessing the full land as promised *(Deut. 30:9; Amos 9:11 14)*

It has to be known, and it is evident that Israel has neither possessed the promised land as set out in *Gen. 15:18 and Numb. 34:1-12,* in line with the unconditional Abrahamic covenant, nor have they just yet, until the completion of the full cycle of the

Palestinian Covenant. These events are also beyond the Mosaic Covenant, the underlying cause of the disobedience.

Israel is still in the third dispersion, and though return has gradually begun, the full cycle of their return will happen when the gentile nations who oppressed them are judged by the Lord and the throne of King David is restored.

TOKEN

The token under the Abrahamic and Mosaic Covenants, basically the religious worship with a High Priest representing the people before God and the cutting of animals to provide cover for sins in atonement and anticipation of the major sacrifice at the cross, was retained. Then Joshua, who led the children of Israel into the promised land, revived the circumcision shortly after they crossed the Jordan River, preparatory to entering the land.

The two foregoing covenants (the 5th and the 6th) could be likened to subjecting the collected data under conventional research to further scrutiny and testing to highlight its integrity, suitability, and reliability for the intended purpose.

DAVIDIC COVENANT (7TH)

This is the 7th Covenant and the penultimate in the series of a diligent search for the seed of the woman proclaimed in Genesis 3:15, as well as separating the godly seed from the ungodly. Separation is the bedrock of godliness in holiness.

Sitting in this 7th position makes this covenant closer to the goal and more definitive on many fronts and frontiers. In line with our strategic research approach, the search is here narrowed to a tribe (Judah) and a family (David's).

The family of David, the second king of Israel, was chosen by God, thus laying credence to the truth that the first Adam failed while the second Adam, Jesus, would do it.

HIGHLIGHTS:

FORMATION: *(2 Samuel 7:8-17)*
Parties: God Almighty on one side, David and his household on the other, with a view on Christ as the Son of David in the flesh.

THE PROMISE

It is a four-part dimensional covenant in promise as follows:

1. A "house" of posterity, family
2. A. Throne," i.e., Royal authority
3. A. Kingdom," i.e., sphere of rule
4. In perpetuity, i.e., forever,"

Taking the four together, God, through the mouth of the prophet Nathan, promised to bring out of the house of David a throne with a king that would rule Israel (indeed the whole world) in an everlasting kingdom.

Only Jesus, Who emanated from the royal lineage of King David, perfectly fits into this house of posterity that God promised to build for David when he (David) wanted to build God a temple or a house. Thus, what man builds is temporary, while God builds eternally, though He supports the temporary in righteousness.

CONDITION

Any disobedience to God by any member of David's house would be met with chastisement to whip that one into line. (2 Sam 7:15, Ps.89:20-37; Isa. 24:5; 54:3).

This punishment was invoked on Rehoboam, the son of Solomon, the son of David, who lost ten tribes of Israel to Jeroboam due to the sin of idolatry committed by Solomon, his father. Jeroboam was the son of Solomon's servant who fled to Egypt when Solomon sought to kill him.

Secondly, this sanction was imposed during the captivity of Jerusalem, and Judah was sent on exile to Babylon. (2 Kings 25:1–7)

It is important to note that the chastisement did not revoke the covenant. Instead, Jehovah Himself confirmed it through:

1. An oath anchored on the covenant of day and night (Ps 89:30–37)
2. Renewed by the angel Gabriel to Mary, through Whom Jesus Christ was born, and crowned with thorns in line with the scriptures

Yet, scriptures confirm that the same Jesus Who was crowned with thorns will return as King of Kings and reclaim His father's throne to reign forever. (Luke 1:31–33; Acts 2:29–32; 15:14–17)

It would appear from the foregoing, that the Palestinian and Davidic Covenants run concurrently, with the Davidic being the narrowed path to the finding of the seed of the woman. Both are still subsisting and have flowed over into the next and final covenant, The New Covenant, discussed in the next chapter under foresight, since it stretches beyond the present generation.

TOKEN

As in the previous four covenants, namely the priesthood and sacrifices of animals, which under David attained a record level, especially during the recovery and relocation of the ark of the covenant, the installation of Solomon as king, and the dedication of the temple built by

Solomon the son of David, who became the third king of the whole of Israel,

CHAPTER FIVE

FORESIGHT -THE NEW COVENANT OF GRACE (8TH).

(Now operational but still looking ahead beyond now.)

This is the last of the eight covenants and indeed the first under the New Testament.

The fact that it occupies the 8th position and sits on the 5th chapter of this divine revelation speaks volumes about its spiritual content, depth, nature, and effect on the whole sphere of supernatural sagacity in Kingdom search.

This covenant is usually compared and contrasted with law, mainly under the Mosaic Covenant, evidencing the fact that those before it (seven in number), as previously discussed in the previous two chapters, had law as their dominant parameter.

Only the Abrahamic covenant, which the Israelites rashly rejected, is different because it was God's riches ably conceived in love and conveyed in gracious favour even without a visible condition. Its dispensation of promise was diminished, but the covenant remained intact. Consequently, this New Covenant is anything but legalistic, even though it has not opened us up to lawlessness but to a Spirit-led relationship with God in the law of the Spirit of life that sets us free from the law of sin and death. *(Rom. 8:1-3)*

With the benefit of hindsight and insight already discussed, the new covenant of grace has a good handshake with the Abrahamic covenant, especially with respect to the promises. It reactivates, enhances, and strengthens it.

The implication of this truth is that rejecting God's love, plan, and purpose, will, wisdom, wishes, works, and wonders, personified and freely given to man in His Son Jesus Christ, is a recipe for disaster in destiny.

Dead or alive, every knee must bow and every mouth must confess that Jesus is Lord.

The intimacy and ultimacy of the new covenant are better appreciated when compared with the Mosaic Covenant, which is the only one that it compares and contrasts in context and content. All other covenants in one way lend credence to the new covenant, save that they wore the garment of law, making unaffordable demands on man in his fallen state, which derailed them.

HIGHLIGHTS OF THE COVENANT OF GRACE: (NEW COVENANT)

Based on Scofield Bible reference notes, slightly adjusted by this revelation, are:

"Better" than the Mosaic Covenant, not morally but efficaciously, from the perspective of man (Heb. 7:19; Rom. 8:3-4)

Established on "Better" (i.e., unconditional) Promises of God without repentance. In the Mosaic Covenant, God demanded righteousness for you to be blessed, saying, "If you will": *(Exod.19:5)*

In the New Covenant, God says, "I will," thus giving us Blessing even while still in sin. We only have to "believe and receive" *(Rom 8:10, 12),* then depart from sin by grace through faith. Not willpower.
Under the Mosaic Covenant, obedience sprang from fear of the law of sin and death *(Hcb. 2:2; 12:25-27):* Under the New Covenant, from a "Willing heart and mind" and love, the Spirit of life in Christ Jesus *(Rom.8:2, Heb.8:10).*

The New Covenant secures a personal revelation of the Lord to every believer *(Heb. 8:11).* Under the

Mosaic Covenant, Israel was dealt with as a nation; a sin by one is a sin for all; failure in one law is failure in all.

The complete oblivion of sin under the New Covenant is indicated: "Your sin I will

REMEMBER no more" *(Heb. 8:12; 10:17; 10:3).* (Emphasis, mine)

Mosaic law stoked and stirred sin in man, leading to his condemnation even to death.

Rests on accomplished redemption *(Matt. 26:27-28; 1Cor. 11:25; Heb. 9:11-12; 9:18-23).*

And secures the perpetuity, future conversion, and blessing of the people of God by choiceIsrael *(Jerem. 31:31-40; 2 Sam. 7:8-18).*

As the 8th covenant, the New Covenant speaks of resurrection and completeness in newness of heart.

There would neither be any other covenant nor generation from the divine order of manifestation before the return of the Lord to fully accomplish the promises of the New Covenant.

In this truth lies the foresight into the heart of God in honouring His promise to deliver a New kingdom to those that sign on to this covenant.

A new kingdom, which is a consolidation of the unconditional love in the promises of God, is and remains the dispensation of this New covenant in testing.

RIGHTEOUS REQUIREMENT. (UNCONDITIONAL)

If you believe in your heart that Jesus Christ was raised from the dead unto righteousness and confess with your mouth that He is the Son of God, the Messiah, unto Salvation, you are saved.

(Rom 10:9-10; John 3:16; 1:12; cf. Is 9:1-7). Hallelujah!

TOKEN

Faith in Christ (Believe in the sacrifice that Jesus made on the cross and His resurrection from the dead). Then partake in Holy Communion to support your faith.

JESUS ON THE CROSS. (See next chapter.)
(I Cor. 1:18; Eph. 2:8-9, 16; Col. 1:20; 2:14; cf. Isa. 53:1-12).

CHAPTER SIX

SUMMARY OF THE HIGHLIGHTS OF THE COVENANTS AND THE RELATION OF   CHRIST TO THEM

This summary is based on the Scofield Reference Bible, slightly adjusted based on revelation to suit the purpose of this project.

1 EDENIC COVENANT

Adam was created and made innocent in the Garden. (Gen.1:26).

His innocence ended with disobedience to God and the introduction of sin (Gen 3:2). This paved the way for the second Man, the "last Adam," Whom scripture recognises as Jesus Christ, Who took the place of Adam *(1 Cor 15:45-47)*.

He took over all that Adam had lost from God. *(Col. 3:10; Heb. 2:7-8)* to rebuild and restore in righteousness.

TOKEN.

Both Adam and Abel offered sacrifices to God. Cain offered an unacceptable sacrifice, pointing to the fact that there are clean and acceptable sacrifices and unclean and unacceptable sacrifices.

2 ADAMIC COVENANT

The Adamic Covenant recognizes the fallen state of man due to sin and reveals a promise to redeem him *(Gen. 3:15)*.

An increase in wilful sin and violence led to the destruction of the whole world by flood, thus confirming the formal end of the dispensation of innocence of the fallen man due to sin *(Gen. 6:5)*.

Jesus Christ was the seed of the woman who was promised to crush the head of the Serpent. *(Gen. 3:15; John 12:31; 1 John 3:8; Gal. 4:4; Rev. 20:10; Mark 6:3)*

TOKEN

God Himself killed an animal, and with its skin, he clothed the Adams, while the blood preserved their lives in atonement. *(Gen. 3:21; Lev 17:11), both temporarily, until the seed to whom the reference was made, Jesus appeared.*

3 NOAHIC COVENANT

After the flood, God entered into a new covenant with Noah and his three children (Gen. 9:1). He renewed the blessings of Adam and introduced the eating of animals, but without their blood. He promised not to destroy the earth again with a flood. Furthermore, he made a rainbow in the sky as a token for this specific promise.

He passed the judicial governance of man to humans, with the power to take the life of any man or beast who takes the life of another man, thus shedding blood.

The human government, which is the dispensation under test here, ended with clear evidence that the human race governed for themselves and not for God in truth.

Comparatively, God did not take the life of man when he rebelled and sinned against Him. But a man takes the life of a man, even when that man is innocent. Cain started it all. God is a merciful and loving God, but man is not, due to his fallen state of sin. The judgment on the tongues at Babel scattered all humans to end human government.

Jesus Christ is the descendant and greatest Son of Shem, by Whom the promises of God were supremely fulfilled. *(Col.2:9.)*

TOKEN

Noah took the best of the animals and fouls and sacrificed them to God, which God perceived and made the covenant not to curse the earth again, as He did under Adam. He also vowed not to destroy the earth again with floods of water, thus preserving nature on earth as long as the earth remains. *(Gen 8:20-22)*. God Himself gave the rainbow as His promise to secure the earth and nature.

4. ABRAHAMIC COVENANT

Following the catastrophic failure of human government, and the separation of the godly race from the ungodly ones, God, chose a man, Abram to work with and rule the earth, with very specific and enticing promises to the nation of Israel that will come out of him.

Thus obedience based promises replaced the judicial sovereignty in human government. The promises are enhanced version of those under the previous covenants.

This dispensation of promise ended when Israel rashly and proudly accepted to do whatever God tells them to do. The Covenant itself remained intact because it was eternal in nature.

Jesus Christ was that SEED to whom the promises were ultimately made and by Whom they were fulfilled. He was the son of Abraham obedient to death. Gen.22:18; Gal.3:16; Eph.2:8

TOKEN:

Circumcision of every male born (free or slave) on his foreskin. Of course there were loads and loads of sacrifice of animals by Abraham & family, as he related with God.

The lamb which was a figure of Jesus was revealed to Abraham in the aborted command to sacrifice Isaac to test his love for and faith in God. (Gen22:12-13.)

5. MOSAIC COVENANT

The rash rejection of the promises of God, made through Abraham out of ignorance, gave birth to this covenant. Exod.19:25

The dispensation of promise was abruptly put on hold and replaced with the dispensation of law. The covenant of God with Abraham, to make him great and preserve Israel that came out of him, however remained sacrosanct and eternal.

Moses was prepared by grace to lead the children of Israrl out of bondage of slavery in Egypt to the promised land.

This covenant saw all men, including the leader (Moses) who was a type of Christ in deliverance, condemned. "For that all have sinned" (Rom3:23) Jesus lived through this covenant without sin, but instead bore the curse of sin for all men (Gal.3: 10-13).

TOKEN:

1.On the eve of their departure from Egypt, they observed the first Passover whereby each family killed a lamb, sprinkled the blood on the four corners of their lintels and are the flesh roasted with bitter herb. That became a memorial statue in perpetuity.
This memorial sacrifice was made a law and was observed while they journeyed to Canaan through the deserts.

2. The appointment of a priest to represent man before God and perform sacrifices for atonement of sins for himself and all Israel.

6. PALESTINIAN COVENANT

The obstinacy of the Israelites in disobedience under the Mosaic law was so alarming that a new covenant that spelt out the conditions under which they would inherit the land in blessings or be cursed and banished was fashioned. That was the origin of the Palestinian Covenant. This covenant was to further check the excesses of the Jews beyond the law under the Mosaic Covenant. It made clear, that sin has incremental consequences and MUST be judged, while God reserves the ultimate power of judgment.

God, however, in consideration of the Adamic and Abrahamic covenants, promised to gather them anywhere they are banished or dispersed on the surface of the earth, restore, convert, and preserve them as a nation. (Deut. 30:3).

Jesus lived obediently under this covenant and was committed, through His death, to fulfilling all aspects of it, especially to saving the Jews and the world. *(Deut 28:1-Deut 30:9)*

TOKEN: As in the Mosaic Covenant above

7. DAVIDIC COVENANT

This covenant narrowed the search for the offspring of the woman to a tribe (Judah), family (David), to bring forth the child. It establishes the perpetuity of David's family on the throne of kingship in Israel. *(2 Sam. 7:16; Matt 1:1; Luke 1:31-33; Rom 1:3)*

Jesus, a descendant of David's family in flesh, is to fulfil this perpetuity in kingdom to the whole world *(2 Sam 7:8-17; Zechariah 7:8; Luke 1:31-33; Acts 15:14-17; 1 Cor. 15:24).*

Jesus is the Seed," Heir," and "King" under the Davidic Covenant *(Matt. 1:1; Luke 1:31-33),* to crush the head of the Serpent that deceived man in the garden of Eden (Gen. 3:15), caused and increased violence on earth in disobedience to God *(Gen. 6:5),* which eventually led to the destruction of the first earth.

He inherited all the promises made to Adam, Noah, Abraham, and their descendants as heirs to the throne and will rule forever as King of Kings, having failed in justice and equity under the human government.

TOKEN:

1. As in 5 and 6 above,

David, Solomon, and most of the Kings of Israel, but Judah in particular, sacrificed thousands and countless numbers of lambs to demonstrate their love for God during the relocation of the ark of the covenant by David and the dedication of the temple by Solomon, not forgetting the marking of the appointed feasts, characterized by the sacrifice of lambs, bulls, sheep, and goats. The unbreakable covenant of Day and night (Jer. 33:20-21)

8. THE NEW COVENANT OF GRACE

As the position '8th' indicates, this is new, not entirely in content but in design and execution. It rests on the sacrifice of the sinless lamb of God, Jesus Christ, that takes away all the sins of the world to secure eternal life for those who believe *(Gal. 3:13-29)*. The blessedness of the Abrahamic Covenant, which Israel rashly rejected but woefully failed under law, previewed this covenant in nature.

No aspect of the new covenant of grace rests on man's responsibility, unlike those preceding it. It is a free gift of God and therefore final, unconditional, sacrosanct, irreversible, and eternal.

The sacrifice of Jesus Christ on the cross is its foundation, while His resurrection and glorification are the indestructible structures in fulfilment and establishment of the eternal Kingdom of God with Jesus as King forever. *Matt 26:28; 1 Cor. 15:25.*

TOKEN:

THE CROSS AND THE HOLY COMMUNION *(Matt. 26:26-29)*

CHAPTER SEVEN

THE SEED OF THE REVELATION (INNERMOST LAYER) THE SPIRITUAL SIGNIFICANCE OF THE HOLY COMMUNION

Having peeled the SHELL of the revelation with the position of Holy Communion in the gospels and epistles, chiseled and cracked the KERNEL of it with the hammer of generational covenants over the ages, and looking at the various aspects of covenant relationships between God and man in the foregoing chapters, the edible SEED is now revealed and hereunder discussed.

This will establish and spotlight what the Lord showed me that Sunday morning: receiving, believing, and practicing faith, which will change the life of every believer.

PRINCIPLES

There is a popular saying among my people that if you despise the old or ancient, you might not recognize the new even if you see it.

Jesus Himself says, Even if you are born again to see the Kingdom of God, you cannot enter unless you are born of water and of the Spirit. *(John 3:3-6)*.

This means that revelations are dynamic and manifestations are on levels.
Again, Jesus says in *Matt. 5:17–18*, I have not come to destroy, but to fulfil and all the laws and prophets must of necessity be fulfilled before the manifestation and accomplishment of the new.

He did; that's the essence and implication of His statement on the cross, "It is finished" *(John 19:30)*.

You may have heard it said or preached that the New Testament was hidden in the Old Testament and the Old Testament revealed in the new.

The implication of all this is that the Word of God, though dynamic, is one and does not change. That's why He is trusted because His promises by His Word are in Christ Yes and Amen; there is no Nay, unto the glory of God by us. *(2 Cor. 1:18-20)*.

Jesus therefore remains the central theme of the Holy Bible's prophecies and manifestations of the truth. The unification of faith in Him, as He told the Samaritan woman in John 4, remains sacrosanct and the main objective of every covenant revealed and reviewed. Scripture further advocates that we should not remove the ancient landmark. Jesus stands at the centre connecting the past and the future together all in Himself to embody and fulfil, hence He is the ancient of days. (Col. 1:17-19; Dan 7:9, 13-22)

Covenants and covenant relationships, as already discussed, therefore remain one incredible vehicle through which God's promises have been conceived, nurtured, and delivered to mankind in truth to establish the faithfulness of God from generation to generation.

Is it necessary then to remind us that **JESUS CHRIST** is **GOD'S COVENANT PERSONIFIED?**
For example, look at the incredulous connection of Jesus right from the seemingly silent first covenant in the garden of Eden, called the Edenic Covenant, all the way through to the open and public knowledge of the New Covenant, which marked the sacrifice of Jesus on the cross of Calvary.

Who would have believed that just as Israel rejected the favour-spiced Abrahamic covenant and ignorantly or arrogantly settled for the life-crushing weight of the law of Moses, they rejected Jesus, the King of Favour, only to know that there is no alternative to Him? Jesus is the anchor of the repackaged and relaunched Abrahamic covenant as the New Covenant, which secures and delivers the blessings of God eternally to both Jews and Gentiles by grace through faith. Anyone who thinks that the rejection which started in the garden through disobedience, is dangeriously deceived and doomed.

We have to be careful what we reject, knowing that God will always have His Way.

When they rejected God as their King and asked for an earthly King like the Kings of the nations, God passed them through the oppressive reign of Saul, who manifested all the qualities and characters of earthly Kings, taking their farmlands, children, silver, and gold to serve his selfish interests for personal purposes.

Is that not the experience of all the nations on earth today?
God supplies in grace and demands in law. The choice is yours. Jesus is Lord and King.

THE COVENANT OF GRACE IS A COVENANT OF HOLY

COMMUNION IN SACRIFICE WITH GOD THROUGH JESUS.

The implication here is that Sacrifice has a way of provoking divine response (acceptance or rejection), going by what happened in the days of Cain and Abel, and blessings of healing and restoration, going by what happened in the Noahic covenant. It is therefore not surprising that God, in consideration of this salutary effect of sacrifice, granted man in his fallen state the right to NOW eat flesh (animals and birds) but WITHOUT THE BLOOD. Before this time, men were only permitted to eat green herbs.

Watch!

Genesis 9:3-4 Every moving thing that liveth shall be meat for you; even as the green herb have I given you all things. But flesh with the life thereof, which is the blood thereof, shall ye not eat.

This eating dimension of the flesh without the blood handed down to Noah and his children was like eating every tree in the garden except the tree of knowledge of good and evil and, of course, the tree of life, handed down to Adam.

The point here is that eating (either as allowed or not allowed) becomes a major part of life in covenant relationships.

Blood, which embodies LIFE in this context, was a picture of the sinless lamb of God, Jesus, which man MUST not eat in his fallen sinful state lest he die. (More on this later.)

From that time on, Sacrifice dotted the whole landscape of the scriptures, in all the covenants, accompanied by eating the permissible parts, while the non-permissible parts, like the blood and entrails, were disposed of in a manner prescribed by God.

It was even instituted as a law and a major part of worship unto God under the Mosaic Covenant, where the various sacrifices that were to be performed and the rules guiding them are well specified.

The dimension of sacrifice that is deeply sacred is the manner of disposal of the blood of the slaughtered animal, which in all cases is sprinkled on the altar.

In a burnt sacrifice, the body is burned either wholly or partially, while in some other forms, like sin offerings and peace offerings, it is eaten in a manner prescribed.

Details are well laid out in the books *(Exo. 12:3-27; Lev 23:5-8; Numbers 9:1-14).*

Sacrifices intensified both in quantity (number of animals slaughtered) and quality (whether it was of sheep, lambs, goats, or bulls of oxen) as the covenants unfolded from generation to generation.

The bloodier, the better, with the oxen or bulls providing the highest blood.

However, we understand that all these sacrifices in the Old Testament were a figure of things to come—the manifestation of the Lamb of God that takes away the sin of man. Remember again that life is in the blood. No amount of the blood of the bulls could atone for the sin of man. They merely covered them until the appearing of the One, the Great High Priest, Who would not offer the blood of bulls and lambs but, as it were, His own blood in one and for all time atonement for the sin of all mankind (Jews and Gentiles).

Watch!

For the law, having a shadow of the good things to come, and not the very image of the things, can never with these same sacrifices, which they offer continually year by year, make those who approach perfect. For then would they not have ceased to be offered? For the worshipers, once purified, would have had no more consciousness of sins.

But in those sacrifices, there is a reminder of sins every year. For it is not possible that the blood of bulls and goats could take away sins. Therefore, when He came into the world, He said: "Sacrifice and offering You did not desire, But a body You have prepared for Me. In burnt offerings and sacrifices for sin You had no pleasure. Then I said, 'Behold, I have come-In the volume of the book it is written of MeTo do Your will, O God.' " Previously saying, "Sacrifice and offering, burnt offerings, and offerings for sin You did not desire, nor had pleasure in them" (which are offered according to the law), then He said, "Behold, I have come to do Your will, O God." He takes away the first that He may establish the second. By that will we have been sanctified through the offering of the body of Jesus Christ once for all. And every priest stands ministering daily and offering repeatedly the same sacrifices, which can never take away sins. But this Man, after He had offered one sacrifice for sins forever, sat down at the right hand of God, from that time waiting till His enemies are made His footstool.

For by one offering He has perfected forever those who are being sanctified.
(Hebrews 10:1-14 KJV).

The above revelation makes a distinctive contrast between all the sacrifices performed all through the seven covenants under the Old Testament of law and the only sacrifice of the offering of Our Lord Jesus Christ on the cross of Calvary as the lamb of God under the New Covenant of Grace in the New Testament.
The former were figures; the latter is real and absolute.

The former could not remove sins and was a reminder of sins each time it was performed under any of the seven covenants.
The latter has perfected forever those who are being sanctified.

The slaughtering of animals and a priest who performs the act, representing the people before God, were the main tokens in those sacrifices, serving as a continuous reminder of sin and the requirement for atonement through blood each year. The bodies of those animals are eaten in a manner prescribed depending on the type of sacrifice, while they are burned wholly or partially in others.

That was a heavy burden economically, socially, and ritually on the parts of the priests and the offenders because any mistake in following the due process, could result in death. A big burden indeed was demanded by God in response to the rebellion and arrogance of man in ignorance. The Chief token under that one for the all-time sacrifice of Jesus through His death on the cross in atonement for ALL sins is His body and bloodshed on the cross. He has therefore, just as it was practised under the animal sacrifices, commanded us to eat both His body and drink His blood. That is, those that are perfected and being sanctified. That's the believers who are now made kings and priests unto God (Rev. 5:10).

That's what we call believing in Him to be saved, backed up and symbolised by the Holy Communion in remembrance of Him as thanksgiving.
It is not a reminder of sin, as was the case under the law with the sacrifice of bulls and animals that could neither take away sins nor perfect any.

Accordingly, a believing man can now eat blood as Holy Communion because sin is no longer imputed to him. He is adjudged cleansed by faith, having confessed Jesus Christ as his Lord and Saviour.

The Holy Communion is a token that attests to that new state in confirmation of the faithfulness of God.

THE HUGE DIFFERENCE IS THAT THE BLOOD, WHICH WAS NOT GRANTED ANY TO TAKE UNDER THE LAW, IS NOW UNDER THE NEW COVENANT OF GRACE ALLOWED TO BE DRUNK AS WE ARE NO LONGER UNDER THE LAW, BUT UNDER GRACE. TO THOSE WHO BELIEVE, CHRIST IS THE END OF THE LAW.

Scripture says life is in the blood *(Leviticus 17:11)*. If any had taken blood before the new covenant and outside the authority of the Lord, that person would have taken judgment upon himself akin to the sin of the garden of Eden and would be cut off.

If the sacrifices of the Old Testament covenants were to be offered in a manner prescribed by God to make them holy, acceptable, and safe, then the Holy Communion should, of necessity, be accorded the sacredness it deserves because it is the body and blood of Our Lord. By any means of assessment and perception, it is more sacred and hallowed than the bodies and blood of lambs and bulls.

Failure to discern this, both in terms of who qualifies to take it and in the manner in which it should be prepared and taken, without making it legalistic but Holy unto God in reverential awe, has consequences, as the Apostle Paul observes and warns. It is here, in this project, reechoed with overwhelming evidence and proofs. That's the function of revelation, or research, in the secular world.

It was with this understanding that the Holy Communion is a sacrifice that must be acknowledged with reverence in order to activate its salutary effect on the spiritual and natural wellbeing of believers that the Lord opened my eyes to see that Sunday morning. It can strengthen the faith of a believer who is a regular partaker and unleash the blessings of healing, wisdom, understanding, and restoration in every area of that believer's life. In this regard, I can testify that my household and I are huge witnesses, all to the glory of God.

If eating in disobedience and at the judgment of God caused the problem in Eden, it is safe to say that eating in strict obedience and at the command of God will do the cure and restoration of what was lost in the Garden after the atonement by Jesus Christ.

Consume in large quantities, in wisdom, the Word and the Holy Communion, both of which are indeed food, and Jesus in figure before and after His sacrifice on the cross to celebrate the victory over sin and its consequences by His stripes and blood. Amen.

See Chapter 12 for the empirical evidence. (Re: The story of the two disciples travelling to Emmaus, etc., and how sin was diminished under the Old Testament by reviewing what was offered for sin and for burnt offerings and peace offerings.)

CHAPTER EIGHT

PROCLAIM, PARTAKE AND CONNECT COMMUNION OF LIFE. PRACTICAL DIMENSION.

IT IS THE DAWN OF A NEW

DAY!

The Holy Communion is a token of the sacrifice Jesus made on the cross of Calvary for the remission of sins.

Partaking in it symbolises that one believes that Jesus truly died on the cross to atone for his sins. He is therefore declaring that he has a share in the inheritance of the saints in Christ. That inheritance is basically more abundant life under the sun and eternal life above the sun when Jesus returns to receive the saints to Himself in the Kingdom of God, which it embodies.

QUALIFICATIONS TO PARTAKE OR PARTICIPATE IN THE HOLY COMMUNION TABLE OF THE LORD, OR CUP OF BLESSING

Confess Jesus Christ as your Lord and Saviour after hearing the message of the gospel, the good news **(See Faith Dedication Page at the end of chapter 12(II)).** Don't take it unworthily.

Let me expatiate a bit on No. 2. There are as many practices and approaches to taking Holy Communion as there are denominations.

This also includes the name we choose to give it. Some call it "Holy Communion", others "The Lord's Supper", or "The Lord's Table," and yet others call it "The Cup of Blessings.". Some of these names derive from Bible versions, and it all depends on which one you are familiar with. The denominations may differ in name and the name they choose to identify with this allimportant faith invocation, but the principles and symbolic significance of the doctrine remain the same. Jesus Christ, Whom the Communion represents, is One from generation to generation.

Whichever name you settle on does not really matter. What matters is your understanding of the importance of what the doctrine is all about in symbolic significance to Christian faith. That's why this project has traced it from creation to date to enlighten our hearts with wisdom and understanding.

I once spoke to a very senior person who was passing through some serious health issues. She is Anglican by denomination, which goes by the name "Anglican Communion." I was inspired to advise her to take Holy Communion daily. But she quietly turned it down, stating that only the priest can administer Holy Communion in their church. Fine, I said, and I told her that it's not written anywhere that only a priest can administer Holy Communion in the sense she implied. That's a presiding, ordained minister of God.

What I know is that only believers should take Holy Communion, and the Bible says we are all priests and kings unto God to reign on earth (Rev 1:6; 5:10).

Besides, when Jesus gave up the ghost at the cross of Calvary, scripture says that the veil dividing the altar into the Holy of Holies and the Holy Place was torn from top to bottom. This means that the deity and laity merged and became one. (Mark 15:38)

However, I must add that, where communion is in a corporate setting involving a number of people, it's imperative that someone, notably the priest or pastor (whichever title your denomination goes with), leads in blessing the elements. (Bread and wine) before it is taken in unison. That's the point the apostle Paul was making.

Before the death and resurrection of Jesus Christ from the dead, sure, under the various sacrifices under the covenant, the Levites, who were the appointed priests to minister unto God, must preside. All that went with the old covenants, The New, brought something new. After all, Jesus, in observing this doctrine, did not hand it to any particular Apostle that we are aware of to share with others in his capacity as the presiding Bishop after Him. Instead, He says, The greatest among you must be a servant of all. "Anyone can lead, serving all."

The second requirement is that we should not take it unworthily.
Before I come to that, let me address yet another myth concerning this strong pillar of faith.

Another strong and devout woman, this time of Catholic faith, called me one day, just as I was doing some teaching on The Holy Communion. She asked me what I thought about a very big Pentecostal Pastor who said that Holy Communion should be taken only at night. I told her that the Pastor in question must have a reason for saying so. Probably because of the word "supper," which is usually the meal before bedtime or evening.

Supper time, technically speaking, starts at 5 p.m. and ends at 7 p.m.

In that case, what Jesus had with His disciples must have been during that time frame, and it should also be noted that the Holy Communion Jesus had with the disciples is different from the Supper. The Scripture says, "After Supper". Could be immediately after, which probably was the case, or much after. Whichever is the case. There is a lot of evidence that most of the communion recorded in the Bible took place at night, without any indication that none took place or must not take place at any other time. It is like the case of whether we should kneel, close our eyes, or not when we pray. These issues are not debate-worthy.

"Reverence is inward and dictates the outward." Being led by the Spirit is what matters.

I told her that I personally do not believe that time is a factor, but desire or inspiration. Are you led to partake? Go ahead, no matter the time.

I advised both women to follow the practices of their respective denominations. Here is why:

If they do anything contrary to what their priests in righteousness preaches and have instituted, the two of them being of the two strongest denominations on earth, would be deemed to be in rebellion.

Scripture says that rebellion or disobedience is like the sin of witchcraft and whatever is not done according to faith is sin. There is also a conscience dimension, doing something that your mind excuses or accuses, making you vulnerable.

Faith is faith when it is solidly focused on God, without wavering, otherwise, it is ruined by doubt.

Now to "Don't eat unworthily"

The Scripture will help us here, not what we think:

Next Chapter

WARNING:

1. DON'T CONFESS JESUS, BECAUSE YOU WANT TO PARTAKE IN THE HOLY COMMUNION. BE INSPIRED TO.

2. HOLY COMMUNION IS A TOKEN OF SALVATION BY JESUS, NOT THE SAVIOUR.

3. BELIEVE & RECEIVE JESUS BY FAITH (REVELATION KNOWLEDGE THAT HE DIED TO SAVE US AND SECURE ETERNAL LIFE IN BLESSING OF THE KINGDOM OF GOD.

4. HOLY COMMUNION WOULD ONLY ENHANCE AND SHARPEN THAT KNOWLEDGE, CONFESSION AND ENRICH YOUR SOUL TO RECEIVE AND MANIFEST MORE.

5. OTHER SUPPORT TOOLS TO HOLY COMMUNION ARE:

a. Prayers, especially in the Spirit.

b. Fasting

c. Reading and studying the word of God.

d. Meditating and Confessing the Word of God.

e. Acting and sharing your faith.

CHAPTER NINE

EXAMINE YOURSELVES FOR UNWORTHINESS.

20. When you meet together, you are not really interested in the Lord's Supper. 21. For some of you hurry to eat your own meal without sharing with others. As a result, some go hungry while others get drunk. 22. What? Don't you have your own homes for eating and drinking? Or do you really want to disgrace God's church and shame the poor? What am I supposed to say? Do you want me to praise you? Well, I certainly will not praise you for this!

23. For I pass on to you what I received from the Lord himself. On the night when he was betrayed, the Lord Jesus took some bread 24. and gave thanks to God for it. Then he broke it in pieces and said, "This is my body, which is given for you. Do this in remembrance of me." 25. In the same way, he took the cup of wine after supper, saying, "This cup is the new covenant between God and his people-an agreement confirmed with my blood. Do this in remembrance of me as often as you drink it." 26. For every time you eat this bread and drink this cup, you are announcing the Lord's death until he comes again.

27. So anyone who eats this bread or drinks this cup of the Lord unworthily is guilty of sinning against the body and blood of the Lord. 28. That is why you should examine yourself before eating the bread and drinking the cup. (1Cor. 11:20-28)

There is a saying that whatever you don't understand, you abuse. That's why the English word
"ABUSE" is made up of two separate words: Abnormal and Use, to get "Abnormal Use Abuse"

Based on the principle of word sound and picture, these are the things I hear and see, present or absent, reading the above passage: confusion, greed, disorder, irreverence, indiscipline, misunderstanding, risk to faith and to life, dishonour, reverence, wisdom, obedience, insight, compliance, etc. That was the setting in the church in Corinth when Apostle Paul had to step in to rebuke and correct them, enlightening their eyes in understanding.

Paul told them that it was an abuse to come into the house of the Lord to partake in the most sacred duty of communing with the Lord through His Holy body and blood, only to rush and eat them as though it was their main supper or dinner. Each one comes in to rush the communion without waiting for others, such that those coming behind would have nothing to eat He condemned that rash behaviour with a stern rebuke. It means they did not have an understanding of what communion was all about. This sharp rebuke again echoes the point that worship in Christian faith is about unified faith in Christ and sharing together.

For this reason, the Apostle Paul counselled them to examine themselves before partaking so as not to eat to condemnation through sickness or even death. "Do you understand what you are doing at all?" Paul seemed to ask them

Here is what we should then understand as eating unworthily or otherwise:

Lack of reverential fear of the Lord, Who should be honoured for His sacrifice in such exercise Lack of understanding of the spiritual context, content, and implications of eating the flesh and blood of Our Lord. Abuse of the sacredness of that solemn exercise by not discerning it as the Lord's body and blood.

The Lord's Supper is not Supper, even if the supper meal is bread and wine, and the sacredness of the Lord is absent in contemplation and understanding.

If rightly observed as prescribed with the reverence and solemnity required, it unleashes health in the body and enlightens the soul in understanding. The opposite is also true, as already indicated above [1–4], each of which is sin because the Lord is dishonoured.

That could lead to condemnation, sickness, and even death.

It is therefore unsafe to say that examining yourself implies that a sinner should not partake in the Lord's Supper or should confess his sins before any priest before he can partake, as if there is a guarantee that the sin is purged when it is confessed to a priest instead of to the one against whom it was committed: God and the person directly involved in the offence, as the Bible stipulates.

However, if there is unconfessed and/or unresolved sin in your consciousness at the time of partaking in the Lord's Supper, the ritual could be an opportune time to make peace privately with the Lord as part of his demonstration of self-examination, not because you want to eat the communion but because you are struck and convicted of your sin, seeing the setting. The Apostle Paul says, quoting the Lord, "Examine yourselves, judge yourselves." He didn't say to confess your sin to others.

If, however, you believe that sharing your fault with a minister or another believer you trust can help your faith in corporate accountability, go ahead! Let it be unto you according to your belief or faith.

In light of this truth, please observe:
The Lord's Supper does not arouse sin in a believer; it is taken in remembrance of the death of Our Lord. A believer is already forgiven, past, present, and future. If you are living in sin, you should examine your confession of Jesus Christ to see if you are actually in the faith.
The Holy Communion is not an ablution for sin. It is a proclamation of our Lord's death to keep us in remembrance of the atonement of our sins once and for all. Meaning that you mourn that death that you and I caused the Lord and celebrate the victory over sin it delivers to us. It helps us to look forward, not backward, as was the case under the law.
This is important because some people think that the sins they commit with their eyes open after professing Christ as their Lord get washed away with the partaking of the Holy Communion. Consequently, they go on sinning and partaking.

That's dishonouring the Lord and disheartening to Him. Such thinking reduces the purpose and potency of the exercise to the Old Testament daily ritual of the sacrifice of bulls to atone for sins, as their eyes were closed to what lay ahead.

A quick review of the practice in the sacrifices of the old covenant would attest to the fact that it's not just everybody that participated in the preparation and eating of the sacrifice materials, not even touching them.

That sacredness holds when it comes to the eating of the Holy Communion even more reverently.

CHAPTER TEN

GUIDELINES ON COMMUNION MATERIALS

I am not about to dictate what Communion materials we should use.

Again, as already declared under the time and timing of the exercise as well as the authority to administer, the nature of the material (not the components) differs from denomination to denomination.

Ladies would always be ladies, just as it was in the Lord's time, when they made front line news in His ministry. While I was still at work, a lady brought Communion wine for me to buy. When I examined the content, I discovered it has about 5–7% alcohol, with Communion wine boldly written on it.

I turned it down, looking at it with that kind of holy eye as though she had committed a sacrilege, arguing that it has alcohol.

The Lady told me that there was nothing wrong with it. Communion wines usually contain a little alcohol, including the ones they use in their church, she boldly asserted without flinching. I vehemently refused. I was young in faith then.

When I reviewed the scriptures, I discovered that what she said was true even in the old Bible days.

The Apostle Paul said in the scripture we reviewed in chapter nine that "some of them would be drunk," which means that the wine, usually made from fig fruits, contained some alcohol. Well, this is not to say I fancy alcohol-laden wines for my Communion. To date, I have sourced my Communion materials (bread and wine) from standard shops. The wine is usually alcoholfree, while the bread is white, rounded flakes, certainly without yeast or mold.

There is no Bible-recommended standard. But one can infer the following from general revelations and usage over the years about acceptable standards:

Bread: Preferably yeast and mold-free.

The lamb, to whom this is both an absolute and a figure, was without blemish. Christ, who is the living bread, knew no sin, did no sin, and sin was not found in Him. He was not convicted of any sin except my sin and your sin, which He carried to the cross when the time was ripe. He lived without sin and learned obedience through the things He passed through.

Wine: Preferably non-alcoholic and one with a red colour (light or dark) to evidence the blood of Jesus.

You are not condemned to using one that has a moderate alcohol content of not more than 5-7% volume, but for the sake of the fledgling faith of many, alcohol-free wines, which abound in the market, are preferred and here recommended.

In the event you can't afford customised communion bread and wine, any biscuit and soft drink of red colour can be served. That's at an individual level. In fact, in the event of an emergency, when the enemy is raging and panting like a bear after the water brooks, water and even normal bread can serve. Speak to them and call them what you are led to call them: the body and the blood of Jesus, respectively.

"It is the priest that sanctifies the altar, not the altar, but the priest." The Word of God is the sanctifier when spoken in faith. (John 17:17)

CHURCH LEVEL

Depending on the size of the church and convenience, Communion wine carriers and Communion bread bowls should be purchased in their numbers to move Communion materials around.

Church workers should be trained on the service of Communion materials without chaos, just as waiters are trained in hotels to serve meals diligently and professionally.

Only believers are qualified to prepare, serve, and partake in the Lord's Supper.

Non-believers MUST not partake unless they have been led in the confession of Jesus Christ as their Lord and Saviour. Besides, they must be briefly told the significance of the Lord's Supper.

THE COMMUNION SETTINGS: INDIVIDUALS AND FELLOWSHIP GROUPS

One of the frequently asked questions is whether Communion should only be taken in church.

The setting Apostle Paul described in 1 Cor 11 was a church setting, but we also know this:

And all the believers met together in one place and shared everything they had. They sold their property and possessions and shared the money with those in need. They worshipped together at the Temple each day, met in homes for the Lord's Supper, and shared their meals with great joy and generosity-all the while praising God and enjoying the goodwill of all the people. And each day, the Lord added to their fellowship those who were being saved. *(Acts of the Apostles 2:44-47 NLT)*

With the above in mind, a group or an individual can partake in the Lord's Supper in a private home and/or a place chosen for fellowship, e.g., an hotel or public place.

The believer or group of believers is the church, not the church building.

Accordingly, there is nothing weird about taking Communion in private homes or public places by individual believers and/or groups of believers, provided they observe the basic protocol of self-examination.

If it is a group of believers, one must take charge to ensure order and discipline, as already outlined.

In such a group setting, it's important that the service of the materials starts with the bread and then the wine.

All will partake at the same time after the blessing is pronounced with a very short prayer by the one in charge.

The significance of this is that the communion symbolizes our unity as one in the faith and as One body, though many, in Our Lord Jesus. We eat the same bread and drink from the same cup. Oneness and unity are key in observing this ritual, the absence of which attracted that rebuke to the Corinthian Church, which Jesus alluded to in that discourse with the Samaritan woman in John 4.

CHURCH LEVEL

As already indicated, this has to be in the church building or a designated public place where a program is taking place.

A high level of diligence and Spirit-led professionalism has to be deployed in administering the Communion materials.

Remember, It Is the Lord's body and should be so discerned and treated. To this effect, the Communion table would have been set up hours before the church service that precedes it begins, on the day chosen to serve the communion.

The communion cups would have been fitted into their carriers, with wine poured into them. They should not be filled to the brim to avoid spilling over to the ground, considering that they will be carried (It's our Lord's precious blood).

The bread, too, would have been poured into the bread bowls, which should be hollow and deep to avoid it sliding and falling out. (It's our Lord's body.) It must not be trampled. Moses was not spared; he struck him twice.

The whole set-up should be covered with a plain material (preferably white or blue) while the service lasts and until the Supper is served. (White and blue colours have the spiritual significance of purity and righteousness.) Look up to the skies; what colours do you usually see covering us from the elements? White and blue, of course. They turn black during rainstorms to indicate danger.

When the service of communion is up and due, the pastor in charge will do the following: Make an altar call for those who want to receive Jesus as their Lord and Saviour, not because they want to receive Holy Communion but because it is safer to do so.

Briefly explain the significance of the Lord's Supper, adding that only believers are entitled to partake for obvious reasons.

Say a corporate prayer of thanksgiving for the sacrifice Jesus made on our behalf. This should be done while the cup and bread are unveiled by removing the material covering them.

The church workers earmarked to serve would file out, standing in front of the altar, while the pastor in charge took steps 1–3 above. A sense of order and sacredness must be observed. The pastor in charge would announce that members should wait with their materials when they receive them until they are told to partake.

The Pastor in charge could take it as he takes step 3 or wait to take it with the whole congregation. He should do as the Spirit leads him.

The serving church workers should take turns carrying the wine carrier in one hand and a bowl of bread in the other and head to their earlier assigned area of coverage. In some cases, these functions are separated between two officers, with one carrying the bread and the other the wine. Whatever is confusion- and burden-free is encouraged.

One or two senior members of the pastorate or deacons should oversee the carriage by the church workers to avoid confusion. It all depends on the size of the church.

The pastor, who would be getting feedback from the officers in charge as to the coverage, would announce it openly, asking any that had not received it to indicate by a shout or raise of hand. When the indication is that all have received their materials, the pastor in charge simply says:

PARTAKE IN THE CUP OF BLESSING OF OUR LORD AND BE BLESSED BY THE LORD! (Say as you are led to invoke the blessing.)

The Pastor would have acknowledged in step 3 that the bread is the body of our Lord, sacrificed for us on the cross, and the blood is the cup of the new covenant, shed for the remission of our sins.

The Congregation would respond:

AMEN! AND TAKE THE BREAD FIRST FOLLOWED BY THE WINE

All these could be spiced up with renditions of solemn hymns or songs of praise in the background, in quiet worship by the choir, fitting for the message of the occasion, which is solemnization in dedication unto the Lord of glory.

The church workers would have their bigger bowls ready to collect the empty wine cups from members immediately after the Lord's Supper for cleaning and safekeeping until the next time around.

The above procedure is largely a Pentecostal approach.
The Catholics and the Anglican Communion have their own ancient methods, which are highly professional and diligent, too.

For example, the Catholics dip the bread in the wine, and the priest serves by putting it in the mouths of the communicants that file to receive one after the other.

This is the method the Lord used in serving Judas, as recorded by Saint John. (I am not implying negativity or negativism here.)

CHAPTER ELEVEN

EMPIRICAL, BIBLICAL, AND CONTEMPORARY EVIDENCES OF THE SALUTARY EFFECTS OF THE HOLY COMMUNION

John 15:21-27

But all these things will they do unto you for my name's sake, because they know not him that sent me.

If I had not come and spoken unto them, they had not had sin: but now they have no cloke for their sin.

He that hateth me hateth my Father also.
If I had not done among them the works which none other man did, they had not had sin: but now have they both seen and hated both me and my Father.

But this cometh to pass, that the word might be fulfilled that is written in their law, They hated me without a cause.

But when the Comforter is come, whom I will send unto you from the Father, even the Spirit of truth, which proceedeth from the Father, he shall testify of me:

And ye also shall bear witness, because ye have been with me from the beginning.

You see, you remain in the dark concerning anything and everything until you receive wisdom and understanding through teaching or revelations by the enlightening of the eyes of your inner man to illuminate your understanding concerning God and His Holy Son, Jesus Christ.

Then, you receive his Spirit, which we lost due to sin, that is the enlightenment in illumination.

This is true of everything about God, including the doctrine of Holy Communion.

Revelation changes anything and everything, to reveal enhancements in type, time and establish new trends to guide actions in relationships.

In this chapter, I highlight biblical and contemporary testimonials with respect to partaking in the Lord's communion.

BIBLICAL (THROUGH THE AGES)

Having established that taking the Holy Communion is a form of marking a sacrifice Jesus made on behalf of humanity, it is therefore safe to say that it is also a form of dedication or consecration to the Lord as the temples of God that we are.

By it, the believer reminds himself that he has been set aside as Holy to the Lord, to serve and honour the Lord.

The Lord showed me from the scriptures eight principal consecrations or dedications set up for the dedication of the people and the altar to God. I said principal because there were many more over the ages, but the ones revealed to me are major and epic.

Our concern here is to see the leadership, preparation, context, and contents of the dedication, as well as the impact on the people in terms of the blessings it provoked.

DEDICATION OF THE ALTAR IN THE DESERT BY MOSES
1st DEDICATION - (UNITY)

Moses was the first High Priest of Israel.

Numbers 7:84-89 This was the dedication of the altar, on the day when it was anointed, by the princes of Israel: twelve chargers of silver, twelve silver bowls, and twelve spoons of gold: Each charger of silver weighed an hundred and thirty shekels, each bowl seventy: all the silver vessels weighed two thousand and four hundred shekels, after the shekel of the sanctuary: The golden spoons were twelve, full of incense, weighing ten shekels apiece, after the shekel of the sanctuary: all the gold of the spoons was an hundred and twenty shekels.

All the oxen for the burnt offering were twelve bullocks, the rams twelve, the lambs of the first year twelve, with their meat offering: and the kids of the goats for sin offering twelve.

And all the oxen for the sacrifice of the peace offerings were twenty and four bullocks, the rams sixty, the he goats sixty, the lambs of the first year sixty. This was the dedication of the altar, after that it was anointed.

THE RESULT

And when Moses was gone into the tabernacle of the congregation to speak with him, then he heard the voice of one speaking unto him from off the mercy seat that was upon the ark of testimony, from between the two cherubims: and he spake unto him.

THE ARK OF GOD RESETTLED IN JERUSALEM BY DAVID:

2nd DEDICATION (DIVINITY)

David was the second King of Israel. (Saul, the first king, failed to honour the altar of God, just as the first man failed to honour God, but the second Adam did.)

David built houses for himself in the City of David; and he prepared a place for the ark of God, and pitched a tent for it. Then David said, "No one may carry the ark of God but the Levites, for the Lord has chosen them to carry the ark of God and to minister before Him forever." And David gathered all Israel together at Jerusalem, to bring up the ark of the Lord to its place, which he had prepared for it. He said to them, "You are the heads of the fathers' houses of the Levites; sanctify yourselves, you and your brethren, that you may bring up the ark of the Lord God of Israel to the place I have prepared for it. For because you did not do it the first time, the Lord our God broke out against us, because we did not consult Him about the proper order." So the priests and the Levites sanctified themselves to bring up the ark of the Lord God of Israel. And the children of the Levites bore the ark of God on their shoulders, by its poles, as Moses had commanded according to the word of the Lord. So David, the elders of Israel, and the captains over thousands went to bring up the ark of the covenant of the Lord from the house of Obed-Edom with joy. And so it was, when God helped the Levites who bore the ark of the covenant of the Lord, that they offered seven bulls and seven rams. David was clothed with a robe of fine linen, as were all the Levites who bore the ark, the singers, and Chenaniah the music master with the singers. David also wore a linen ephod. (I *Chronicle 15:1-3, 12-15, 2527 NKJV)*

So they brought the ark of God, and set it in the midst of the tabernacle that David had erected for it. Then they offered burnt offerings and peace offerings before God. And when David had finished offering the burnt offerings and the peace offerings, he blessed the people in the name of the Lord. Then he distributed to everyone of Israel, both man and woman, to everyone a loaf of bread, a piece of meat, and a cake of raisins. (I *Chronicles 16:1–3 NKJV)*.

Notice that no SIN OFFERING was mentioned, even if it was implied. This is revelatory and spiritually symbolic.

THE RESULT

On that day David first delivered this psalm into the hand of Asaph and his brethren, to thank the Lord: Oh, give thanks to the Lord, for He is good! For His mercy endures forever. And say, "Save us, O God of our salvation; Gather us together, and deliver us from the Gentiles, To give thanks to Your holy name, To triumph in Your praise." Blessed be the Lord God of Israel From everlasting to everlasting! And all the people said, "Amen!" and praised the Lord. *I Chronicles 16:7, 34–36 NKJV*

(ALSO READ 1 Chronicles 15 and 16 entirely, for the whole prayer of thanksgiving by David as well as the order and continuous worship he instituted before and after the resettlement of the Ark.)

DEDICATION OF THE TEMPLE BY SOLOMON IN JERUSALEM:

THE 3RD DEDICATION (TRINITY)

Solomon was the third King of Israel. All of Israel was united in this. When God was to create man, who is a temple, He involved God the Son and God the Holy Spirit. (Gen1: 26)

Now Solomon assembled the elders of Israel and all the heads of the tribes, the chief fathers of the children of Israel, to King Solomon in Jerusalem, that they might bring up the ark of the covenant of the Lord from the City of David, which is Zion. Therefore all the men of Israel assembled with King Solomon at the feast in the month of Ethanim, which is the seventh month. So all the elders of Israel came, and the priests took up the ark. Then they brought up the ark of the Lord, the tabernacle of meeting, and all the holy furnishings that were in the tabernacle. The priests and the Levites brought them up. Also King Solomon, and all the congregation of Israel who were assembled with him, were with him before the ark, sacrificing sheep and oxen that could not be counted or numbered for multitude. Then the priests brought in the ark of the covenant of the Lord to its place, into the inner sanctuary of the temple, to the Most Holy Place, under the wings of the cherubim. For the cherubim spread their two wings over the place of the ark, and the cherubim overshadowed the ark and its poles. (I Kings 8:1–7 NKJV)

THE RESULT & WHAT FOLLOWED

And it came to pass, when the priests came out of the holy place, that the cloud filled the house of the Lord, so that the priests could not continue ministering because of the cloud; for the glory of the Lord filled the house of the Lord. Then Solomon spoke: "The Lord said He would dwell in the dark cloud. I have surely built

You an exalted house, And a place for You to dwell in forever." And so it was, when Solomon had finished praying all this prayer and supplication to the Lord, that he arose from before the altar of the Lord, from kneeling on his knees with his hands spread up to heaven. Then he stood and blessed all the assembly of Israel with a loud voice, saying: "Blessed be the Lord, who has given rest to His people Israel, according to all that He promised. There has not failed one word of all His good promise, which He promised through His servant Moses. May the Lord our God be with us, as He was with our fathers. May He not leave us nor forsake us, that He may incline our hearts to Himself, to walk in all His ways, and to keep His commandments and His statutes and His judgments, which He commanded our fathers. And may these words of mine, with which I have made supplication before the Lord, be near the Lord our God day and night, that He may maintain the cause of His servant and the cause of His people Israel, as each day may require, that all the peoples of the earth may know that the Lord is God; there is no other. Let your heart therefore be loyal to the Lord our God, to walk in His statutes and keep His commandments, as at this day." Then the king and all Israel with him offered sacrifices before the Lord. And Solomon offered a sacrifice of peace offerings, which he offered to the Lord, twenty-two thousand bulls and one hundred and twenty thousand sheep. So the king and all the children of Israel dedicated the house of the Lord. On the same day the king consecrated the middle of the court that was in front of the house of the Lord; for there he offered burnt offerings, grain offerings, and the fat of the peace offerings, because the bronze altar that was before the Lord was too small to receive the burnt offerings, the grain offerings, and the fat of the peace offerings. At that time Solomon held a feast, and all Israel with him, a great assembly from the entrance of Hamath to the Brook of Egypt, before the Lord our God, seven days and seven more days—fourteen days. On the eighth day he sent the people away; and they blessed the king, and went to their tents joyful and glad of heart for all the good that the Lord had done for His servant David, and for Israel His people. *I Kings 8:10-13, 54-66 NKJV.*

(Please read the entire 1 Kings 8, to acquaint yourself with the prayer of supplication of King
Solomon like the Psalms
of his father David in
1Chronicle 16) Also read
II Chronicles 5:4-7, 11-14

NKJV for the same account.

Notice again here, that sin offering was muted.

DEDICATION OF THE HOUSE IN JERUSALEM ON THEIR RETURN AFTER CAPTIVITY-TURNING POINT. 4TH DEDICATION (STABILITY)

The elders of the Jews (North, South, East, and West) came together to rebuild and dedicate the altar, helped by heathen kings at the command of God.

Then Tattenai, governor of the region beyond the River, Shethar-Boznai, and their companions diligently did according to what King Darius had sent. So the elders of the Jews built, and they prospered through the prophesying of Haggai the prophet and Zechariah the son of Iddo. And they built and finished it, according to the commandment of the God of Israel, and according to the command of Cyrus, Darius, and Artaxerxes king of Persia. Now the temple was finished on the third day of the month of Adar, which was in the sixth year of the reign of King Darius. Then the children of Israel, the priests and the Levites and the rest of the descendants of the captivity, celebrated the dedication of this house of God with joy. And they offered sacrifices at the dedication of this house of

God, one hundred bulls, two hundred rams, four hundred lambs, and as a sin offering for all Israel twelve male goats, according to the number of the tribes of Israel. They assigned the priests to their divisions and the Levites to their divisions, over the service of

God in Jerusalem, as it is written in the Book of Moses. *Ezra 6:13-18 NKJV.*

THE RESULT & OUTLOOK THEREAFTER

And the descendants of the captivity kept the Passover on the fourteenth day of the first month. For the priests and the Levites had purified themselves; all of them were ritually clean. And they slaughtered the Passover lambs for all the descendants of the captivity, for their brethren the priests, and for themselves. Then the children of Israel who had returned from the captivity ate together with all who had separated themselves from the filth of the nations of the land in order to seek the Lord God of Israel. And they kept the Feast of Unleavened Bread seven days with joy; for the Lord made them joyful, and turned the heart of the king of Assyria toward them, to strengthen their hands in the work of the house of God, the God of Israel. *Ezra 6:19-22 NKJV.*

Notice that the sin that was undercover under the 2nd and 3rd dedications in Jerusalem was uncovered through the wanton disobedience of the Jews, as well as the blasphemy of the name of God in the lands where they had been driven, and had to be atoned for on their return. This is the second fulfilment of the Palestinian Covenant, which was the 6th Covenant. (See Chapter 3, No. 6). Besides, the sin atonement had to be reopened to cover the gentiles, who are now part of this universal dedication. (Ths revelation is privately given to me in this project, and not anywhere I know of before now)

OFFERING OF CHRIST AS THE PASSOVER LAMB

5TH DEDICATION (GRACE)

Then came the Day of Unleavened Bread, when the Passover must be killed. And He sent Peter and John, saying, "Go and prepare the Passover for us, that we may eat." So they said to Him, "Where do You want us to prepare?" And He said to them, "Behold, when you have entered the city, a man will meet you carrying a pitcher of water; follow him into the house which he enters. Then you shall say to the master of the house, 'The Teacher says to you, "Where is the guest room where I may eat the Passover with My disciples?" ' Then he will show you a large, furnished upper room; there make ready." So they went and found it just as He had said to them, and they prepared the Passover. When the hour had come, He sat down, and the twelve apostles with Him. Then He said to them, "With fervent desire I have desired to eat this Passover with you before I suffer; for I say to you, I will no longer eat of it until it is fulfilled in the kingdom of God." Then He took the cup, and gave thanks, and said, "Take this and divide it among yourselves; for I say to you, I will not drink of the fruit of the vine until the kingdom of God comes." And He took bread, gave thanks and broke it, and gave it to them, saying, "This is My body which is given for you; do this in remembrance of Me." Likewise He also took the cup after supper, saying, "This cup is the new covenant in My blood, which is shed for you. But behold, the hand of My betrayer is with Me on the table. And truly the Son of Man goes as it has been determined, but woe to that man by whom He is betrayed!" "But you are those who have continued with Me in My trials. And I bestow upon you a kingdom, just as My Father bestowed one upon Me, that you may eat and drink at My table in My kingdom, and sit on thrones judging the twelve tribes of Israel." *Luke 22:7-22, 28-30 NKJV*. See Rev.20:4)

Recall the Greek word for covenant, which is 'diathēkē' from the root word 'diatithêmia, of which the verb in the passive voice is 'diatithemi, meaning to arrange or dispose of one's own affairs by assignment, compact, or bequest.

This verb was used by our Lord in the above scripture (Luke 22:29), wherein in this covenant of the Holy Communion, He divided His body (dia) through (tithemi) an intensive covenant with the disciples by which in figure He assigned, bestowed, or bequeathed

His Kingdom, bequeathed to, or bestowed on Him by the Father, in love sharing with believers.

This would manifest in the dispensation of the Kingdom as outlined in the 8th dedication, highlighted below, after the Believers' dedication (6th) and the Davidic dedication (7th), the penultimate sacrifice with Jesus and believers ruling for one thousand years. (The Millennium
Rule)

So each time we take Holy Communion as believers, we attest to this truth in the proclamation of eternal life in Christ, delivered to us by faith, plus more abundant life now under the sun.
(John10:10b).

This will remain in force until the Kingdom of God, which it points to, manifests and is delivered on the return of the Lord.
Let this mind be in you each time you partake.

THE RESULT

IMMEDIATE

And when they had sung a hymn,
they went out to the Mount of Olives.
Matthew 26:30 NKJV.

AFTER HIS RESURRECTION

Let's review the live testimony of two disciples of Jesus traveling to Emmaus, whose confusion about the testimony of the resurrection of Jesus was cured by encountering Jesus and partaking in the Holy Communion administered to them by Him.

Please take time to read Luke 24:1–53 (especially 13–35) to connect to this:

Luke 24:25-32 Then he said unto them, O fools, and slow of heart to believe all that the prophets have spoken:
Ought not Christ to have suffered these things, and to enter into his glory?

And beginning at Moses and all the prophets, he expounded unto them in all the scriptures the things concerning himself.

And they drew nigh unto the village, whither they went: and he made as though he would have gone further.

But they constrained him, saying, Abide with us: for it is toward evening, and the day is far spent. And he went in to tarry with them.

And it came to pass, as he sat at meat with them, he took bread, and blessed it, and brake, and gave to them.

And their eyes were opened, and they knew him; and he vanished out of their sight.

And they said one to another, Did not our heart burn within us, while he talked with us by the way, and while he opened to us the scriptures?

ADVISORY AND INSPIRATIONAL WORD OF COUNSEL

1. When you read the word, ask the Lord to abide with you. He would by His Spirit.

Look forward to the abiding presence of the Lord through His Spirit to open your eyes to seeing Him and knowing Him through the scriptures. That's faith-seeing and knowing Jesus through

His word, the scriptures. After all, He is the Word of God made flesh. *(John 1:14)*

Holy Communion enhances this understanding. It is the equivalent of the sacrifice of bulls and lambs under the Old Testament, but much more sacred, for it is the proclamation of the death and resurrection of Our Lord, to which those sacrifices were mere figures.

Jesus disappeared from their view because the flesh had to leave or be closed for the Spirit to be revealed. Start every sacred exercise with a prayer to herald a spiritual atmosphere of sacredness.

They found strength to travel back to Jerusalem that same night because the Holy Spirit, spiked by the communion, energized them.

5. The Holy Spirit did not appear to abide with us until Jesus was glorified. Once Jesus departed, He came ten days later to abide in and with us forever and teach us everything concerning Jesus and all He did and taught us. (CF Luke7:38-39)

DEDICATION OF MAN TO CHRIST FOR SALVATION
6TH DEDICATION (MAN)

COMMENCEMENT

That Sunday evening the disciples were meeting behind locked doors because they were afraid of the

Jewish leaders. Suddenly, Jesus was standing there among them! "Peace be with you," he said. As he spoke, he showed them the wounds in his hands and his side. They were filled with joy when they saw the Lord! Again he said, "Peace be with you. As the Father has sent me, so I am sending you." Then he breathed on them and said, "Receive the Holy Spirit. If you forgive anyone's sins, they are forgiven. If you do not forgive them, they are not forgiven." *John 20:19-23 NLT.*

NOTE: Those two disciples were most probably in this meeting when Jesus walked in to dedicate them. It was at the meeting that they were first baptised with the Holy Spirit and became saved and safe. Before then, they were not.

CONFIRMATION AFTERWARDS

On the day of Pentecost all the believers were meeting together in one place. Suddenly, there was a sound from heaven like the roaring of a mighty windstorm, and it filled the house where they were sitting. Then, what looked like flames or tongues of fire appeared and settled on each of them. And everyone present was filled with the Holy Spirit and began speaking in other languages, as the Holy Spirit gave them this ability. At that time there were devout Jews from every nation living in Jerusalem. When they heard the loud noise, everyone came running, and they were bewildered to hear their own languages being spoken by the believers. They were completely amazed. "How can this be?" they exclaimed. "These people are all from Galilee, and yet we hear them speaking in our own native languages! Here we are-Parthians, Medes, Elamites, people from Mesopotamia, Judea, Cappadocia, Pontus, the province of Asia,

Phrygia, Pamphylia, Egypt, and the areas of Libya around Cyrene, visitors from Rome (both Jews and converts to Judaism), Cretans, and Arabs. And we all hear these people speaking in our own languages about the wonderful things God has done!" They stood there amazed and perplexed. "What can this mean?" they asked each other.

Acts of the Apostles 2:1-12 NLT.

SUBSEQUENTLY: DEDICATION OF BELIEVERS UNTO CHRIST. FORMAL MESSAGE - BY APOSTLE PETER

"God raised Jesus from the dead, and we are all witnesses of this. Now he is exalted to the place of highest honor in heaven, at God's right hand. And the

Father, as he had promised, gave him the Holy Spirit to pour out upon us, just as you see and hear today. For David himself never ascended into heaven, yet he said, 'The Lord said to my Lord, "Sit in the place of honor at my right hand until I humble your enemies, making them a footstool under your feet."' "So let everyone in Israel know for certain that God has made this Jesus, whom you crucified, to be both Lord and Messiah!" Peter's words pierced their hearts, and they said to him and to the other apostles, "Brothers, what should we do?" Peter replied, "Each of you must repent of your sins and turn to God, and be baptized in the name of Jesus Christ for the forgiveness of your sins. Then you will receive the gift of the Holy Spirit. This promise is to you, to your children, and to those far away—all who have been called by the Lord our God." Then Peter continued preaching for a long time, strongly urging all his listeners, "Save yourselves from this crooked generation!" Those who believed what Peter said were baptized and added to the church that day— about 3,000 in all.

Acts of the Apostles 2:32-41 NLT

LATTER MESSAGE -BY APOSTLE PAUL

I beseech you therefore, brethren, by the mercies of God, that you present your bodies a living sacrifice, holy, acceptable to God, which is your reasonable service. And do not be conformed to this world, but be transformed by the renewing of your mind, that you may prove what is that good and acceptable and perfect will of God. *Romans 12:1-2 NKJV*

Therefore purge out the old leaven, that you may be a new lump, since you truly are unleavened. For indeed Christ, our Passover, was sacrificed for us. Therefore let us keep the feast, not with old leaven, nor with the leaven of malice and wickedness, but with the unleavened bread of sincerity and truth. *I Corinthians 5:7-8 NKJV.*

This is ongoing and will continue until the return of The Lord to repair the broken and ruined Tabernacle of David as promised, which is the 7th dedication. (Is. 9:7; 54:1–5; Amos
9:11–12).

Being the 7th, it marks the end of all dedications after the judgment of the nations that will gather against the Holy City, Jerusalem, the seat of power of Jesus (Rev. 20:4-6). Then the 8th, which is the revealing of the Kingdom of God, the New Jerusalem, after the Millennial reign of

Jesus with the saints over
whom the second death
has no power, (See Rev.
20:5–18, 21:1–8)

JUST AHEAD AND SHORTLY BEFORE THE 8TH DEDICATION (THE NEW JERUSALEM BEING AWAITED)

Revelation 19:1-9 And after these things I heard a great voice of much people in heaven, saying, Alleluia; Salvation, and glory, and honour, and power, unto the Lord our God:

For true and righteous are his judgments: for he hath judged the great whore, which did corrupt the earth with her fornication, and hath avenged the blood of his servants at her hand.

And again they said, Alleluia. And her smoke rose up for ever and ever.
And the four and twenty elders and the four beasts fell down and worshipped God that sat on the throne, saying, Amen; Alleluia.

And a voice came out of the throne, saying, Praise our God, all ye his servants, and ye that fear him, both small and great.

And I heard as it were the voice of a great multitude, and as the voice of many waters, and as the voice of mighty thunderings, saying, Alleluia: for the Lord God omnipotent reigneth.

Let us be glad and rejoice, and give honour to him: for the marriage of the Lamb is come, and his wife hath made herself ready.

And to her was granted that she should be arrayed in fine linen, clean and white: for the fine linen is the righteousness of saints.

And he saith unto me, Write, Blessed are they which are called unto the marriage supper of the

Lamb. And he saith unto me, These are the true sayings of God.
See Matt.26:29, 42; 27:34, 48)

He drank the bitter vinegar mixed with gall on our behalf here on earth, that we may drink the fruit of the vine with Him in the marriage supper in His Father's Kingdom. Amen.

INSPIRED EXPLICATIONS

- General Commentries.
- Summary

There were four temple dedications in the Old Testament in anticipation of the cross (dedications under Moses, then under King David and King Solomon, and finally by the elders of Israel in collaboration with gentile kings who supported them).

Another four are in the New Testament, which was reviewed above.
In all, eight dedications (five already undertaken, one ongoing, and two in view)

The 5th dedication resulted in the offering of Jesus on the cross as the Passover lamb that takes away the sins of the whole world, covered under the old sacrifices and dedications. (John 1:29) The disciples prepared the Passover, and the lamb was sacrificed in figure through the Holy Communion as Jesus celebrated that last Passover, the last in this lower world, the earthly Jerusalem.

The next and best with Him would be in the new Jerusalem, in the Marriage Supper of the Lamb. (The 8th). This could be a physical celebration or a state of spiritual fulfilment of the promises made, or even both. We know in part.

The actual sacrifice of Jesus through crucifixion took place on the cross, carried out by a joint conspiracy of both the Jews and the Gentiles. No one is therefore with excuse, as all partook in the sacrifice, not according to the will of man but according to the determinate counsel of God.

Compared with the four that preceded it, as a covenant of grace, here is what you see:

The first was performed and presided over by a high priest. (Moses)
The second and third were performed and presided over by Israelite Kings (King David and King Solomon).

The fourth and last under the old covenant were jointly prepared and presided over by the elders of Israel and the children of Israel with support from the Persian kings, commanded by God, though the priests were in the background.

In the 4th dedication, both the earthly priests and kings were muted and made spiritually insignificant, replaced by the elders and children of Israel. This is to make the point that in the rebuilding of the temple (See seventh and eighth), it's all about Christ, the elders, and the redeemed saints, here represented by the leaders and children of Israel that returned from captivity. (See Rev 4:4, 19:4-6). Only Jesus, the King of Kings, and the Great High Priest are visible. All the kingdoms of the earth have been swallowed up by the Kingdom of God, with Jesus as King. (Rev 11:15)

In terms of context and content of the sacrifices, the first was held outside Jerusalem, which attests to their universality, but the second, third, and fourth were all held in Jerusalem, indicating their peculiarity to Israel. The 6th, 7th, and 8th are universal, though they will first have their base in Jerusalem before terminating in the New Jerusalem, a new world.

When the first was dedicated, sin was present and imputed; hence, there was a sacrifice of goats for the sin offering.

During the 2nd and 3rd centuries, only bulls and lambs were offered in burnt and peace offerings, as sin was muted and they were deemed clean by God, Who ordered the building of the temple. This was the figure of a believer dedicated to Christ. (See John 13:10; 15:3).

Sin was again atoned for in the 4th because sin reentered leading to the captivity or dispersal and had to be judged after the captivity on their return. The participation through the support of the genile kings had to be acknowledged and atoned for by the killing of goats in sin offering. This is a picture of the 7th dedication and what will happen during the rebuilding of the Davidic throne by Jesus and the judgment of the nations that will encompass the Holy City to fight the chosen people of God. (See Rev. 20.)

The death of Jesus Christ marks the end of all animal sacrifices, as the blood of Jesus fully atones for the sins of all those who believe and dedicate their lives to Him. It also ends every sin's consequences-sickness, disease, curses, sorrows, etc.

This 5th partly points to the 6th in reality and the 7th and 8th in figure until Jesus returns to fulfil them all.

No sin is imputed to a true believer. Is all paid for (past, present, and future) in righteousness. Only the sacrifice of thanksgiving in praise and worship of the King of Kings is required. (Rev.19-20). However, sinners would be judged for their sins according to their works in the white throne judgment. (See John 13:11; Rev 20:4; 21:8)

The rebuilding of the fallen tabernacle of David and its dedication would set up the millennium rule and intensify the reign of Jesus, leading to the final judgment of the devil, the beast, and sinners, while the saints are rewarded with citizenship in the Kingdom, ruling with Jesus as priests and kings. No sacrifice. The blood of Jesus still speaks in judgment and defence.

The unveiling of the kingdom: no sacrifice, no sin, no devil, no judgment Only righteousness in celebration.

It is important to point out that between the first dedication by Moses and those that followed and the anticipated final dedication, there are some other dedications, which in the old testament were basically feasts in renewal of the covenant or cleansing of the defiled or polluted temple by some of the Kings of Israel or the heathen nations during war. Example Dedication in the days of King Hezekiah (2 Chr. 29)

Under the New Testament, these dedications take the form of our Sunday services or faith programs, where we rededicate our lives to Jesus Christ in worship and thanksgiving to God in anticipation of the return of Jesus to fulfill the last two Mega dedications.

Accordingly, the Holy Communion we take, reading, preaching the word, prayers, fasting, and evangelism are all aids to those dedications unto God through Jesus and part of them in the maintenance of our faith until His return.

However, the Lord showed me the eight highlighted as the dedications that marked the turning points and shaped the covenant relationships between God and man as integral parts of those eight covenants shared. By them, we remind ourselves that we are sanctified, set apart to serve God and humanity in righteousness.

GENERAL COMMENT AND SUMMARY

In Summary, the glory of the kingdom became more visible and revelatory, and though sin reentered and increased, grace intensified and much more abounded unto a perfect day. Believers who would appear before the judgment seat of Jesus (not the white throne judgment) would be rewarded and crowned as long as their names were found in the book of life.

Watch!

2 Corinthians 5:10

For we must all appear before the judgment seat of Christ; that every one may receive the things done in his body, according to that he hath done, whether it be good or bad.

Romans 5:15

But not as the offence, so also is the free gift. For if through the offence of one many be dead, much more the grace of God, and the gift by grace, which is by one man, Jesus Christ, hath abounded unto many.
Romans 5:20

Moreover the law entered, that the offence might abound. But where sin abounded, grace did much more abound:

The fifth, which was the sacrifice and birth of grace, resulted in the sacrifice or dedication of Jesus as the Passover Lamb, which was prepared by the disciples.

The sixth, which is the believers' sacrifice and dedication, is self-sacrifice (present yourselves a living sacrifice) helped by the Holy Spirit unto Jesus, the Great High Priest, the Altar.

The seventh is the fulfilment of the Davidic Covenant, which secured the house, family, and throne of David forever through his 'seed', 'Heir', King of Kings, Jesus Christ, Who is already dedicated and crowned. That would be the rebuilding of the tabernacle of David, which has fallen down and is in ruins (Is. 9:7; 54:1–5; Amos 9:11-12).

This marks the end of dedications before the Kingdom (New Jerusalem) is unveiled.

Watch!

Amos 9:11-14 In that day will I raise up the tabernacle of David that is fallen, and close up the breaches thereof; and I will raise up his ruins, and I will build it as in the days of old:

That they may possess the remnant of Edom, and of all the heathen, which are called by my name, saith the LORD that doeth this.

Behold, the days come, saith the LORD, that the plowman shall overtake the reaper, and the treader of grapes him that soweth seed; and the mountains shall drop sweet wine, and all the hills shall melt.

And I will bring again the captivity of my people of Israel, and they shall build the waste cities, and inhabit them; and they shall plant vineyards, and drink the

wine thereof; they shall also make gardens, and eat
the fruit of them.

Acts 15:16-18 After this I will return, and will build
again the tabernacle of David, which is fallen down;
and I will build again the ruins thereof, and I will set it
up:
That the residue of men might seek after the Lord, and
all the Gentiles, upon whom my name is called, saith
the Lord, who doeth all these things.

Known unto God are all his works from the beginning
of the world.
As indicated in the above scripture, Jesus would set up
the tabernacle, which is expected to be the seat of His
throne here on earth for the millennial rule (one
thousand years), together with the raptured saints
who would return and rule with Him. It is otherwise
called the first resurrection.

Watch!

Revelation 20:4-6 And I saw thrones, and they sat upon
them, and judgment was given unto them: and I saw
the souls of them that were beheaded for the witness
of Jesus, and for the word of God, and which had not
worshipped the beast, neither his image, neither had

received his mark upon their foreheads, or in their hands; and they lived and reigned with Christ a thousand years.

But the rest of the dead lived not again until the thousand years were finished. This is the first resurrection.

Blessed and holy is he that hath part in the first resurrection: on such the second death hath no power, but they shall be priests of God and of Christ, and shall reign with him a thousand years.

It is not clear if the Holy Communion would continue for believers since Jesus would be present bodily. However, since this 7th dedication is primarily the rebuilding of the ruined Tabernacle of David, incorporating the deliverance of the Jews, the unclean sacrifices by the gentile nations would continue until they were judged.

The eighth and final dedication is the unveiling of the Kingdom of God, with the Messiah living together with the saints forever after the final judgment of the devil, called death, cast into the lake of fire, burning with fire and brimstone together with the beast and false prophet, who deceived the nations. There would be no more sickness, death, sorrow, etc. The second death has no power over the saints in this kingdom.

Watch!

Revelation 20:5-15 But the rest of the dead lived not again until the thousand years were finished. This is the first resurrection.

Blessed and holy is he that hath part in the first resurrection: on such the second death hath no power, but they shall be priests of God and of Christ, and shall reign with him a thousand years. And when the thousand years are expired, Satan shall be loosed out of his prison,

And shall go out to deceive the nations which are in the four quarters of the earth, Gog and Magog, to gather them together to battle: the number of whom is as the sand of the sea.

And they went up on the breadth of the earth, and compassed the camp of the saints about, and the beloved city: and fire came down from God out of heaven, and devoured them.

And the devil that deceived them was cast into the lake of fire and brimstone, where the beast and the false prophet are, and shall be tormented day and night for ever and ever.

And I saw a great white throne, and him that sat on it, from whose face the earth and the heaven fled away; and there was found no place for them.
And I saw the dead, small and great, stand before God; and the books were opened: and another book was opened, which is the book of life: and the dead were judged out of those things which were written in the books, according to their works.

And the sea gave up the dead which were in it; and death and hell delivered up the dead which were in them: and they were judged every man according to their works.

And death and hell were cast into the lake of fire. This is the second death.

And whosoever was not found written in the book of life was cast into the lake of fire.

Revelation 21:1-8 And I saw a new heaven and a new earth: for the first heaven and the first earth were passed away; and there was no more sea.

And I John saw the holy city, new Jerusalem, coming down from God out of heaven, prepared as a bride adorned for her husband.

And I heard a great voice out of heaven saying, Behold, the tabernacle of God is with men, and he will dwell with them, and they shall be his people, and God himself shall be with them, and be their God.

And God shall wipe away all tears from their eyes; and there shall be no more death, neither sorrow, nor crying, neither shall there be any more pain: for the former things are passed away. And he that sat upon the throne said, Behold, I make all things new. And he said unto me, Write: for these words are true and faithful.
And he said unto me, It is done. I am Alpha and Omega, the beginning and the end. I will give unto him that is athirst of the fountain of the water of life freely.

He that overcometh shall inherit all things; and I will be his God, and he shall be my son.

But the fearful, and unbelieving, and the abominable, and murderers, and whoremongers, and sorcerers, and idolaters, and all liars, shall have their part in the lake which burneth with fire and brimstone, which is the second death.

Give HIM praise! Hallelujah!
ARE YOU READY?
MARANATHA.

DEDICATION OF ONE'S LIFE TO CHRIST

Father, thank You for sending Your Son Jesus Christ to die and pay for my sins. I receive Him as My Lord And Saviour.

I believe He rose again from the dead to deliver Your Life to me, which I now believe and receive.

Thank You Jesus, Come and live in me.

I am a new creation. Amen.

OTHER BOOKS BY THE AUTHOR

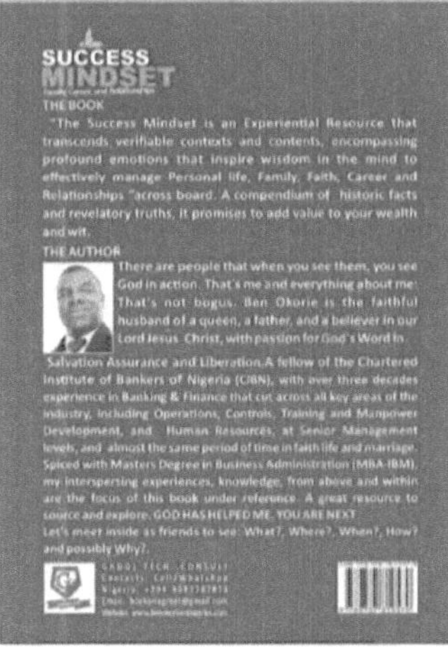